COACHED BY THE LORD IN THE SCHOOL OF ADDICTION

DUSTIN HAWKINS

ISBN–13: 978-1-945431-11-1

Printed in the United States of America.

dustin@workoutaddictionrecovery.com
801-648-3705
1070 E. 5600 S., Ogden, UT, 84405

CONTENTS

PREFACE

I'm truly grateful for the Church of Jesus Christ of Latter-day Saints, and also for the great men and women who serve in such a beautiful cause. I became active in the Church nearly eight years ago from being addicted to amphetamines and opiates, and since my decision to do so, my life has never been the same.

Early on, I was challenged by a group of sister missionaries to read and study the words of modern-day prophets. I began studying the writings of these men with intensity because I was interested in capturing the perspective on life that they were carrying. I also began with an intensity to read and study the scriptures. I found that the scriptures taught me in a different way, and my study therein became serious and life-changing.

I never did traditional rehab for my addiction recovery program. Instead, I have been participating in the Church of Jesus Christ's repentance process. Yes, I have participated in the rooms of AA, worked with a therapist, and have done the Church's addiction recovery program, but most of my spiritual work has been done from me being active in the Church. I was eventually given a calling to teach. I studied the doctrine of the Church. Most importantly, I tried to act on the doctrine that I was learning. I worked with a bishop, started bringing my kids to church, and on a later date baptized my wife—our family was eventually sealed in the Ogden Utah Temple.

My life's work has since become to help those who struggle with drug and alcohol addiction. I chose to take on the responsibility of writing this book so that I could attempt to help those who struggle with drug and alcohol addiction to find peace and sobriety by using the Atonement of Jesus Christ in the same way that I am. I figured that it was important for me to share what little I have come to know concerning the healing powers that take place when one is participating in the gospel of Jesus Christ's repentance process.

For those who may be reading this book who are, or are not, members of the Church—I would ask you to consider being open and not to get offended. I would consider myself a novice when it comes to the Church's doctrine, so please give me a pass if you find some weakness in my writing. I tend to get very bold and declarative at times during this book, but just keep in mind that I am passionate about helping people to find this new way of life, and I believe that it's sometimes necessary for the one who struggles with addiction to take on hard advice from time to time. Parts of this book do provide that hard advice—but it was hard advice that I had to take on in my own recovery. Therefore, I'm not in any way being judgmental, since I myself have gone through it.

I use a lot of scripture references in this book, so please don't get frustrated if you don't quite understand that type of language. I felt it was very important to add these scriptures to the book with hopes of them working for you in your recovery. There is a certain power that attends scripture study, and my hope is that you will capture the beautiful spiritual experience that happens when we "feast upon the words of

Christ" (2 Nephi 32:3). There is power in scripture study, and those who finds themselves in the practice of it daily will most likely gain a new perspective on how to go about doing life.

This book talks of a lifestyle of health that ranges anywhere from capturing spiritual experiences through obedience to the commandments to being healthy in the way of mind, body, and spirit. Take from it what you will, but every healthy practice that is promoted in this book is a true principle. It speaks of an elite way of life that is full of abstaining and competing with ones' self. And when individuals start competing with themselves on the daily by fighting to stay obedient and sober, then oftentimes what follows is a contrite spirit when they end up falling short. This book's goal isn't to make you feel bad about yourself for when you fall short. Instead, it is to help you create awareness around how you act so that you can be less impulsive in your decision making. We have to watch how we act out in the world, or we will be acted upon.

I'm thankful for the leaders of the Church from whom I've studied. They have given me an example of how to act and be in this life. I couldn't have written a book such as this were it not for me studying and reading their books and talks. Neal A. Maxwell has become my favorite gospel writer, but there are plenty of others who have taught me the gospel as well. I'm thankful for the teachings of Boyd K. Packer, Thomas S. Monson, Gordon B. Hinckley, and the many others I have quoted inside this book. In a selfish way, I've always felt that their words and ways of describing how an individual is to capture happiness in this life have always been directed at me. These men are the reason why I came to love the gospel of Jesus Christ in the way that I do. I have leaned on their bright writings when my mind has been filled with darkness. Their words have inspired me to be a better man—a gospel man—even a disciple of Jesus Christ.

I have found it very hard to release a book such as this, because who am I to give advice about how to use the gospel of Jesus Christ to overcome drug and alcohol addiction? I'm no general authority, stake president, or bishop who is seasoned in his understanding of the gospel. I'm just a man who was asked to participate in the gospel experiment to help him overcome his own addictions, and what followed from such participation was a new and improved man who has become more than he ever thought that he could become.

And so I release this book with hopes of it helping somebody in the same way.

ACKNOWLEDGMENTS

To my dad, Brad; my father-in-law, Mike; and to my brothers-in-law, Matt, Austin, and Mike. Gentlemen! I figured the only way I might get you to read Mormon literature was if I wrote it.

"AND YE SHALL KNOW THE TRUTH, AND THE TRUTH SHALL MAKE YOU FREE" (JOHN 8:32)

This book is also for my children to read when they get older—so that they might gain a true understanding of what the gospel of Jesus Christ did for their mom and dad.

ORIENTATION

Before we were born into this world, our Heavenly Father called a Grand Council to present His plan for our succeeding in the game of life (see *Teachings of Presidents of the Church: Joseph Smith* [Salt Lake City: The Church of Jesus Christ of Latter-day Saints, 2007], 209, 511). In this special council, we learned that "[His] work and [His] glory" is "to bring to pass the immortality and eternal life of man" (Moses 1:39). We learned that if we followed His spiritual system here in this life, that we could become like Him, and would experience being resurrected with hopes of one day landing our souls at "the right hand of God in the kingdom of heaven" (Helaman 3:30; see also D&C 132:19–20).

We learned that He would provide an earth for us to compete with ourselves on. "And we will prove them herewith, to see if they will do all things whatsoever the Lord their God shall command them" (Abraham 3: 24–25). And that upon arrival into mortality a veil would be placed over our memories so that we would forget our heavenly home, thus becoming free agents, who are now able to experience the test of life without being influenced by the memory of living with God.

Furthermore, we learned of how our beautiful progression on the "strait and narrow course" (Helaman 3:29) would lead us to experience peace and happiness in this life. However, we also learned of those who would be "wandering in strange roads" (1 Nephi 8:32), being deceived, and thus becoming drug addicts who are "past feeling" (Moroni 9:20). But we understood "that all these things shall give [us] experience, and shall be for [our] good" (D&C 122:7). And that if we successfully made our way through these trials of addiction by using Christ's Atonement, then a great learning experience would take place that would enable us to become those who are "instruments in the hands of God in bringing many to the knowledge of the truth, yea, to the knowledge of their Redeemer" (Mosiah 27:36; see also *Teachings of Presidents of the Church: Spencer W. Kimball*, [Salt Lake City: The Church of Jesus Christ of Latter-day Saints, 2006] 15–16).

In this council, we learned that we would have weaknesses, and how they would lead us to the sins of "the natural man." But if we overcame our weakness and competed with ourselves daily by putting "off the natural man," that a Savior would be provided so that we could overcome our sins and "becometh a saint through the atonement of Christ the Lord, and becometh as a child, submissive, meek, humble, patient, [and] full of love" (Mosiah 3:19).

STOLEN AGENCY: THE SPIRITUAL WAR

In the premortal existence, there was also an epic war in heaven between good and evil. Satan's proposed plan was to enslave humankind by controlling everyone's actions, thus enabling every soul to return to God innocent. But God had a different plan—one that allowed people to make their own choices, suffer from their own mistakes, and learn what would ultimately make them happy. He employed His favorite Son to be the executor of His plan, a Son who would do what He asked and not demand His power. "Father, thy will be done," said Jesus Christ, "and the glory be thine forever" (Moses 4:2).

The Dragon and his followers, or the "stars of heaven" (Revelation 12:3–4), were exiled to Earth as fallen angels—spirits damned by their rebellion without the opportunity for incarnation (see Jude 1:6): "And there was war in heaven: Michael and his angels fought against the dragon; and the dragon fought and his angels, And prevailed not; neither was their place found any more in heaven. And the great dragon was cast out, that old serpent, called the Devil, and Satan, which deceiveth the whole world: he was cast out into the earth, and his angels were cast out with him" (Revelations 12:7).

Adrift without purpose or opportunity for evolution, their sole objective became to enact the plan that Satan had originally proposed: slavery, bondage, and unhappiness, without the ability to think for ourselves, progress, or to even know the difference. We, on the other hand, chose God and freedom. We "sang together" and "shouted for joy" at the opportunity to be born on Earth and participate in mortality—a test designed by God to help His creations spiritually evolve (Job 38:7). God "formed the earth and made it; he hath established it, he created it not in vain, he formed it to be inhabited" (Isaiah 45:18).

DEVELOPING FAITH

I have chosen to develop faith in this doctrine because it gives me an understanding of my purpose here in life. If I know where I was before the test of life and that it was my choice to participate in the test, then it makes it easier for me to understand why life is so hard and challenging. Why, then, do I struggle with this disease of addiction? Well, maybe in my long life in the premortal existence I had developed patterns of behavior that made me more prone to being an addict; and so I chose to enroll in this life test (the School of Addiction) to see if I could overcome that which has always been apart of my character; so that I could one day make it back to live with my Heavenly Father, being spotless, pure, and able to receive the full measure of glory that only comes to those who pass the test.

The Lord said, "My people must be tried in all things, that they may be prepared to receive the glory that I have for them, even the glory of Zion; and he that will not bear chastisement is not worthy of my kingdom" (D&C 136:31).

It seems that a great many in the premortal existence, including Abraham, were set apart because of their obedience: "And God saw these souls that they were good, and he stood in the midst of them, and he said: These I will make my rulers; for he stood among those that were spirits, and he saw that they were good; and he said unto me: Abraham, thou art one of them; thou wast chosen before thou wast born" (Abraham 3:23).

Jeremiah was likewise foreordained to be a prophet and was called as a mortal to declare the word of the Lord: "Then the word of the Lord came unto me [Jeremiah], saying, Before I formed thee in the belly I knew thee; and before thou camest forth out of the womb I sanctified thee, and I ordained thee a prophet unto the nations" (Jeremiah 1:4–5).

Maybe Einstein, Gandhi, and other brilliant leaders and inventors started developing their brilliance, leadership, and talents in the premortal existence in the same way, but then chose to further their brilliance by "[keeping] their first estate" (Abraham 3:26) and thus enrolling in the test of life so that they could be challenged in other ways—ultimately to help mankind grow towards their Creator. The same goes for all the prophets, any other historical figure that has played an influential role in the tale of the world, and even us. This belief system gives us purpose and will help us to understand our role in the great plan of happiness. This belief system can help us to overcome our addictions and fears because it will remind us of where we once were and where we hope to go.

THE SPIRITUAL SYSTEM

The gospel of Jesus Christ is that spiritual system upon Earth that can lead an individual to the type of change needed to "land their souls, yea, their immortal souls, at the right hand of God in the kingdom of heaven"

(Helaman 3:30). Through the gospel of Jesus Christ, we have an older Brother who provided us with a perfect example of how to successfully compete in the game of life. He felt our pains and the darkness of our minds. He showed us the type of life that we should live in order to capture the abundant life. He has given us the perspective that our performance in this life determines where we will land in the next life, thus holding us accountable for the way that we act. Christ forgave everybody, even those who persecuted Him. He served by healing the sick and causing the lame to walk. He was the Good Samaritan who helped the poor. He was the wise counselor and coach who led by example and taught by parable. He was patient and fearless when the storms of adversity came after Him and His disciples. He was meek, humble, submissive, patient, and quiet in His behavior. He never talked behind people's backs or spoke ill of anybody. He abstained from temptation and was our perfect exemplar on how to live a beautiful life.

By choosing to develop faith in Jesus Christ, you will be given a perfect example of how to act in this life. He is the son of God and creator of "worlds without number" (Moses 1:33). He was born into mortality to teach us His doctrine and to take our sins upon Him. He enacted a plan of salvation that would allow us to repent, and our "sins and [our] iniquities will [He] remember no more" (Hebrews 8:12). And if we follow His lead and try to develop His character attributes, we will be blessed beyond measure and will inherit a beautiful life—not only in the here and now, but also beyond the grave.

I've battled with the disease of addiction for many years now, and the only treatment that has worked for me is the gospel of Jesus Christ. I've worked with hundreds of people in an effort to lead them to change, and the ones who are open enough to try the gospel experiment are those who have the best chance at overcoming their addictions. What I can tell you is this: if you want to change, then the gospel of Jesus Christ can help. However, Christ's system for leading people to change takes "works" (James 2:20), so anything that you take away from this book needs to be put into action. Here we go!

CLASS 1
ABSTAIN

"Abstain from all appearance of evil."
Thessalonians 5:22

Congratulations on making the decision to change and become free from drugs and alcohol. These first few weeks are going to be rough, and I imagine you are going to be physically sick and full of hopeless and depressive thoughts. No matter how bad your physical withdrawals and your mental state become, you must abstain from that substance that has been blinding you for all of these years. It will get better, I promise! You aren't the only one who has gone through this pain. I, myself, have been through it, along with countless others who have fought this very same fight. Abstain from the substance! I'll say it again—abstain from the substance! If you can't abstain, then we can't move on to the new life of which I'm hoping to teach you. I can very well teach you a way of life that is so fun and enjoyable that your cravings and mind struggles will become nonexistent. But it takes this first step of you abstaining from that substance which has brought you so much misery. Abstain, no matter the pain!

During this time of detox, go ahead and lay low, drink plenty of water, eat protein, vegetables, and some fruit, and by all means be a reader. Your mind is going to be irritated and sad, so it's important that you put beautiful self-help literature into your mind so that thoughts of hope can develop. Put Christ and all of His beautiful doctrine into your system, and then pray to God and ask Him to make you strong in mind, body, and spirit. Pray, read, and then go for a walk and ponder what you have been reading about. And then go back inside to read and pray some more so that you can go for another walk and have something further to ponder about. Keep this cycle of reading, praying, and walking going, and before long you will begin to feel hopeful. This ritual cannot be a one-time try; it has to be done daily and with focus, for "He becometh poor that dealeth with a slack hand: but the hand of the diligent maketh rich" (Proverbs 10:4).

I had a red couch in my house that had all of my books surrounding it. I would read, pray, and then walk and ponder about what I had been reading, all while carrying a continuous prayer in my heart. When returning home, I would make my way back to the red couch for more reading, praying, and studying about Christ. My mind craved happiness and peace, and these books about Christ provided me with a unique hope that all would be well if I kept aligning my life with His. Days, weeks, and finally months went by with this beautiful routine, and it is still something I do to this day. I have to keep refreshing my testimony of the Christ, or I run the risk of traveling back into my old behaviors. In my prayers, I would ask God to help me keep going on this newfound path of studying, pondering, meditating, and praying. These were things I had never done before. However, I could tell that they were true practices, ones that were sure to lead me to a higher plane spiritually, mentally, emotionally, and even physically.

LAY LOW AND GO TO MEETINGS

During this time, you need to slow your life down and lay low. If you are out running around and acting busy, that tells me you don't want to get sober and probably aren't sober. I'm not promoting you to be lazy, so don't get that twisted. And I realize that many of you may be working and have responsibilities; but what I'm saying is that you should be laying low, going to AA and ARP meetings, reading, walking, praying, going to bed early, waking up early, and exercising daily.

The AA meetings will help you to abstain and is free treatment, so you have no excuse not to attend one every day. You can head into those meetings being humble and willing to learn from others on how they have found sobriety. You also can share about how you are doing if you feel like it. You might surprise yourself and find out that you like getting things off of your chest. All of the people in these rooms are going through, or have been through, exactly what you are currently going through. These rooms are a safe place for you to get honest. Don't be hardened against these rooms by acting like you have all the answers, because you don't! The only way the spirit of these rooms can heal you is if you walk into them being softened and ready to learn.

As I myself traveled into these rooms for help, I found a spirit of charity residing there that felt good. As I listened to the AA message and heard others share their story, I began to feel a sense of belonging, because I now wasn't alone. I never went to traditional rehab, and so these meetings were my rehab, along with the Church of Jesus Christ of Latter-day Saints. My study of Christ—along with what I was learning in my church, AA, and ARP meetings—is what makes up my spiritual foundation today, which is the foundation that keeps me grounded and sober. You, too, can build your life "upon the foundation of the apostles and prophets, Jesus Christ himself being the chief corner stone" (Ephesians 2:20).

HIGHER POWERS

My higher powers became God, the Eternal Father; His Son, Jesus Christ; and the Holy Ghost, which in Christianity makes up the Godhead (Article of Faith: 1:1). It was easy for me to get into Christ and AA meetings because I was at an all-time low and was convinced that I was never going to be happy again. I had always heard that God and Christ could help people to change, so I leaned on what I had heard and made a place in my heart and soul for faith to start working.

In my prayers, I pray to my Heavenly Father in the name of Jesus Christ. I then try and align my way of life with that of Jesus Christ's. "Hear my prayer, O Lord, and let my cry come unto thee" (Psalms 102:1). I try and emulate His character, and when I'm doing good, I can feel the Holy Ghost implanting charity and peace within my mind and heart. When I offend the teachings of Christ by being loud in my behavior and selfish, or even through relapse, I can feel the Holy Ghost leave my system. I then become scared and fearful once again.

For me, that charity given to me by the Holy Ghost when I'm dialed in to living Christ's lifestyle is what keeps me sober. When I feel charitable and want to help others, I have no desire to escape my problems, stress, or boredom, since my mind is filled with happiness and thoughts of gratitude for even the simple things in life. Paul taught, "Now the God of hope fill you with all joy and peace in believing, that ye may abound in hope, through the power of the Holy Ghost" (Romans 15:13).

For example, think about how it is that you feel when you are in the service of others and are living a morally clean life, when compared to sitting in some parking lot to pick up or being strung out on drugs or addicted to pornography. The former is a charitable high given to us by the Holy Ghost, and the latter is pleasure-seeking behavior that is linked to the Dragon, or Satan.

So you can see by this example how one can tell the difference between that feeling of charity that comes from God and that feeling of shame and selfishness when chasing after the Dragon and his worldly highs. It's important to understand the difference between these two spirits so that you can come to crave those charitable highs instead of the world's highs. From one who has experienced both highs, I'm here to testify to you that God's highs are the far better highs. But in order to capture these highs, you must quit those fast and immediate practices of the world, and that is no easy feat.

If you are seeking after happiness by seeking after pleasures, then you will escape happiness altogether. One cannot find true happiness by participating in the world's fast pleasures because there is no solid ground to stand on inside that type of fast and immediate lifestyle.

Elder James E. Talmage describes the difference between pleasure and happiness:

> The present is an age of pleasure-seeking, and men are losing their sanity in the mad rush for sensations that do but excite and disappoint. . . . Happiness includes all that is really desirable and of true worth in pleasure, and much beside. . . . Happiness leaves no bad after-taste, it is followed by no depressing reaction; it calls for no repentance, brings no regret, entails no remorse; pleasure too often makes necessary repentance, contrition, and suffering. (*Improvement Era*, Dec. 1913, 172–73)

THE MOMENTS

True happiness is found in those moments when your young three-year-old son helps you to mow the lawn with his little toy lawn mower, or when that same son tells you that he loves you after he had been telling you that he hated you for making him go to bed. It's when your wife gives you that hug of appreciation for being a good father and husband. It's the realization of how much your little girl reminds you of your wife, and how thankful you are to be the man in their life who has the opportunity to provide for them and to protect them. It's the struggles with money, followed by the appreciation for the simple things in life that don't involve money. It's the stress, followed by appreciation; it's the hard times, followed by the good times, where you then appreciate the good times more fully because of the fact that you endured through the hard times without running to the escape. It's the belief system that God is protecting you and your family.

It's the slow summer Sunday afternoon spent with the family out working and playing in the yard, where you stop often to appreciate the beautiful day, even thanking God for such a day and the way of life that He has led you and your family to live. It's the sunburn on your son's face that he got from running in the sprinklers. It's the family prayer at night before bed, and it's the personal prayer in the morning where you ask God to watch over and protect the ones you love. It's the getting up in the middle of the night with your little girl when she's had a bad dream. It's the working together with your wife in growing your little family. It's teaching your kids the importance of staying away from the bad things of this world and how to use God in their life so that they can experience for themselves the full, abundant life—never having to experience the dark way of life as you once have.

It's the moments when true joy is whispered into your mind, advancing overwhelming thoughts of gratitude that lead to a growth of your soul. These are the high moments that can only be captured in the sober life.

I tell you these things so that you might get an idea of the important role that God plays in my life and the perspective (moments) that He has helped me to capture. Now it's your turn to exercise faith in Jesus Christ and to participate in the gospel experiment. But remember, you must practice a lifestyle of health: mentally, spiritually, and physically. If not, the still, small voice of the Holy Spirit will get drowned out by the noise of the world.

DAILY ACCOUNTABILITY AND GROWTH

Each night before bed, I perform a step 10 (personal inventory) in my prayers, where I repent of my shortcomings and ask for help to be better at where I'm weak. I also feel saddened and contrite for when I offend the Holy Spirit by not acting in the way that Christ has taught me. Now that I have lived the commandments and have experienced the peace of His beautiful way of life, I feel saddened when I sin out of my own love for Him. What used to be selfish adoration of myself has now turned into emulation and adoration for Him. I take comfort in the words of Moroni: "But as oft as they repented and sought forgiveness, with real intent, they were forgiven" (Moroni 6:8).

You need to get to the point where you love Jesus Christ so much that you don't want to break His commandments! I told Heavenly Father, in what has been many prayers, that I would turn my entire life over to Him and that He could make of me what He will. I have felt like clay in the potter's hand, and every time more adversity strikes in my life, I realize that I'm being presented with an opportunity to learn and grow. I know that God won't give me any challenges that He doesn't think I can handle. Therefore, I welcome adversity, because that means I'm being provided with an opportunity to grow into the man that God would have me become.

I take further comfort in the words of Paul: "There hath no temptation taken you but such as is common to man: but God is faithful, who will not suffer you to be tempted above that ye are able; but will with the temptation also make a way to escape, that ye may be able to bear it" (Corinthians 10:13).

PRAYER

I learned a powerful lesson one day from my son about the importance of prayer. As a seven-year-old playing tackle football, he was scared before one of his games. We pulled up to the venue, and I asked him if he wanted to have a prayer experience with me, where I would ask Heavenly Father to protect him in the game and to help him overcome his nerves so that he could relax and have fun in the game. After the prayer, I told my little boy that Heavenly Father would help him because we asked Him in prayer; and that He always has to honor prayers from those who are obedient to His commandments. I watched my little boy's countenance and expression light up with confidence, and I learned on that day that prayer and faith are true. My little boy now had faith that a higher power than himself was going to watch over and protect him during his game, and so it is the same with us. We are our Heavenly Father's children, and He will protect us as we exercise faith in Him by competing with ourselves each day in an effort to follow His commandments.

Give place for prayer in your routine! Walk outside before bed at night and have a conversation with God. Ask Him to keep helping you to abstain. Tell Him your worries, fears, and stresses, and then ask Him to help you walk through them without taking a substance. Create prayer experiences for yourself all day long, and watch what will happen to your life. You will start seeing the hand of God working in your life, and then you will gain faith that He is working for you. He's proud of you for having the courage to quit something that is hard to quit. Most people will just coast along in this life, being drifters with no desire to abstain from the fast escape—but not you!

CHRISTLIKE CHARACTER

The human species wants everything now. They want to feel better now without having to put in the work to achieve the lasting high—true happiness. True happiness is granted to those who are willing to work through their struggles without looking for the quick fix. Everyone is attracted to the pill that quickly makes them feel happier, safer, and more proactive. However, that pill cannot grow a character in the right direction. Only God's lifestyle of health can do that.

We can grow our character upwards if we seek after God's highs. But if we want to be told how to capture these highs, then we must be in constant communication with Him. In the morning, we pray; all day long we pray; and at night, we pray. We must make a conscious effort to take time out of our day to have a prayer experience! We might think to stop and go for a quick walk so that we can talk to God outside and in nature. We might hop into an empty room at work to get down on our knees and pray. We might pray when driving or when any free time arises. It takes a conscious effort to get into a relationship with God. After a while of this type of praying and abstaining, you will start getting ideas put into your head on how to capture God's highs. He might lead you to have a jogging experience while listening to beautiful sounding music. He might lead you for a walk on the scenic trails while listening to His scripture words, and then to send out healthy text messages to those you love and for whom you are thankful for. Over time, He will put His charity high in you (the Holy Ghost), which is the greatest of all highs since it's the "pure love of Christ" (Moroni 7:47).

A KID AGAIN EXPERIMENT

The lifestyle of Christ means trying to become as an innocent child again. Do you believe that you can one day become as an innocent child? Don't you remember what it was like to be free from drugs and alcohol? Take a minute and travel back to the time of when you were an innocent child. Do you remember how you looked and felt? Were you running around and playing? Were you laughing and enjoying the simple things in life?

All people, regardless of what they say, had a time in their life where they were free from drugs, alcohol, depressive thoughts, and anxieties. Again, do you believe that you can travel back to this innocence?

Currently, I'm participating in this experiment myself, and have found overwhelming peace, and have even experienced smells of my childhood youth. Often, I go back to places of old where I had good experiences as a child so that I might capture the nostalgia of a time well spent.

You, too, can walk back through some old neighborhoods and parks in an effort to capture this special form of nostalgia. If we can catch a glimpse of who we once were, then our memories of a time well spent away from drugs and alcohol can work for us, even helping us to move forward as we look backward.

It starts with getting some time away from all substances so that your brain can heal, therefore allowing some light to travel back into your mind and soul. All of us were born with this "light of Christ" (Moroni 7:18–19), but as we grew further away from our childlike selves and more towards the world with all of its quick escapes, we have since pushed this important light out of us, and have become "past feeling" (1 Nephi 17:45).

COMPETE WITH YOURSELF

It starts with slowing your life down and allowing your problems to come after you. This means having a determination to change your life in a big way. If you aren't determined and willing to abstain from all addictive substances, then your life will continue to go in the circle of jail, rehabs, probation, and finally down to the grave.

It's going to get hard in your head when you first pull all of the substances out of your system, which is why you must lean on God for support and guidance. This is where hope comes into play. You need to carry the hope that things will get better as you boldly travel through the shadowy learning experiences of withdrawals, cravings, sadness, stress, depression, and anxiety. It's the hope that on the other side of these shadows lies a "perfect brightness of hope," and a new understanding of how to execute in life (2 Nephi 31:20).

Of course your mind is going to be sad and stressed, and those cravings are going to come after you; but remember, once you let the world back into your system, your life will travel back into the monotonous addiction circle instead of traveling upwards on the "strait and narrow path" (2 Nephi 31:18).

You need to learn to deal with these cravings, or they will always have the upper hand. You have to show them that you can beat them at their own game by not being so quick to pick up. Endure through the cravings, and with just a few wins under your belt, you will gain confidence, and the obsession in your mind will quiet down, in which peace is sure to follow.

You may use the argument of "What's the point in changing your life when it has become this bad?" and it seems so far out of reach. This life is a proving ground and test, and if you carry that attitude, then you will fail indefinitely. There is always time to change! Can you imagine the type of coach and missionary you would become with all of this priceless training that you've had in the School of Addiction? The epidemic of drug and alcohol addiction isn't going anywhere, and the world needs courageous people who have had the courage to change, thus giving way for them to help others to change. If you are looking for purpose, well then, that's your purpose. You are on this planet to see how much of the world you can quit so that you can then teach others how to quit. If this pattern of student to coach could move forward, then we just might make an impact on the world's addiction epidemic. But it starts with you and me, even one step at a time.

EXERCISE YOUR DEMONS

So get moving, and be active in mind, body, and spirit while you are fighting your way through the shadows. If your demons see you exercising and being active, then they will cower down and become less active towards you. Instead of your demons exercising you, you will be exercising them in calisthenics that they aren't in shape for. Walk out your front door and go for a jog or walk while at the same time working on prayer and gratitude the entire way. Look to appreciate scenery so that you might capture a bigger perspective of God's plan for you. You do need to find a power higher than yourself, and nature has a way of telling us just how small we really are.

During this time, search for the belief system that if you abstain from drugs and alcohol, then you will be blessed for your efforts. "There is a law, irrevocably decreed in heaven before the foundations of this world, upon which all blessings are predicated" (D&C 130:20). Picture God cheering you on, with Him having a hope that you will remain on this new path so that He can bless you. Now His hope for you, and your hope in Him, can come together to form a "perfect brightness of hope" (2 Nephi 31:20). This is how hope will help you travel, with success, through these addiction shadows. You now have faith that if you abstain from your past behaviors that God will lead you along on the strait and narrow course.

KEEP A POSITIVE ATTITUDE

Don't let your social and financial position affect your attitude and spiritual condition. I realize that you are in a low spot in all aspects of your life, but such will not be the case six months or a year from now if you will continue to abstain from drugs and alcohol. You've got some learning and growing to do, so put on your reading glasses and go to work! At first, it's going to feel like a maze, where one door opens to yet another dead end. But if you will keep searching for the way, then you will make it out of the dark maze and will soon find yourself on the peaks of sobriety.

There are no better highs than those captured in the sober life. Imagine yourself being free, clear-eyed, and full of health. Imagine yourself looking and feeling better, being able to look people in the eye when having conversations. Imagine getting complimented for how good you look and for the progress you've made on changing your life in a big way. Imagine all of this and more, and then make it all happen. You can't just dream about this mighty change, but you must do this mighty change, which I'm here to tell you will be the hardest thing you've ever done in your life, but it is doable if you truly want it. You have to want this sobriety so bad that you are willing to change everything about yourself.

I came to the realization that I didn't want to take this life for granted anymore, and neither should you. Life is a big deal, and if we want to one day find wealth, stability, peace, and happiness, then we had better get our game faces on and be willing to compete in the big show. Yes, all people's circumstances vary, and some have longer roads to travel than others, but that's still no excuse to coast through this life by staying in hiding behind a substance.

Abstain from the substance regardless of how dark things get inside your head, and just know that things will get better the further away that you get from the substance, but it all starts with you first abstaining from drugs and alcohol so that you can move forward on this beautiful journey of recovery. Seek first to abstain! You can do it! It's so much better on this side.

CLASS 2
SOFTENED

"And behold, I thank my great God that he has given us a portion of his Spirit to soften our hearts."

Alma 24:8

W e cannot do it without God, lest we "fall into transgression [and] be destroyed from off the face of the land" (Jarom 1:10).

Upon starting in the great School of Recovery, we must be open and leave our hard self behind. There is absolutely no room for hardness unless you want to fall hard. If you are one who is always getting offended, acting argumentative, and being controversial, then there is no doubt that you will fail at changing.

Jacob sets a beautiful example by speaking to us "in words of soberness that ye would repent, and come with full purpose of heart, and cleave unto God as he cleaveth unto you. And while his arm of mercy is extended towards you in the light of the day, harden not your hearts" (Jacob 6:5).

The way of life that Christ promoted was beautiful in every way, and His principles and concepts were those of truth. Being humble, patient, hopeful, loving, charitable, virtuous, knowledgeable, temperate, having brotherly kindness, and diligent are just a few of the many attributes that Christ promoted (D&C 4:5–6). Not one person could ever say that having these Christ-like attributes would be a bad thing; which means they are the truest, most important forms of character that a person could hope to capture in this life.

Therefore, we are not in a position to be hardened in the School of Addiction since our sobriety is dependent on how soft we can become. Being one who is offended all of the time is a lame practice. We can make the choice to not get offended so that we can be open to hearing the "still voice of perfect mildness" (Helaman 5:30).

David A. Bednar said, "It ultimately is impossible for another person to offend you or to offend me. Indeed, believing that another person offended us is fundamentally false. To be offended is a choice we make; it is not a condition inflicted or imposed upon us by someone or something else" ("And Nothing Shall Offend Them," *Liahona*, November 2006).

Those of us who are being coached by the Lord will have no problem in admitting that we are powerless and need the help of God to overcome our addictions. Those who will not admit that they have a problem and try and do it alone will end up wandering around in the School of Addiction halls without ever figuring out how to make it to class. We need help from our Head Coach to make it to class, and then we need further help from Him on how to pass the class so that we can move forward "on the strait and narrow course across the everlasting gulf of misery" (Helaman 3:29).

PLAYERS IN THE GAME-OR NOT

The current world that we live in is full of addicts, many of whom need serious help. The epidemic of drug, alcohol, and pornography addiction plays a serious threat to society since the disease divides the family. Lehi, a Book of Mormon prophet, said, "And because he [Lucifer] had fallen from heaven, and had become miserable forever, he sought also the misery of all mankind" (2 Nephi 2:18).

Elder Russell M. Ballard of the Quorum of the Twelve Apostles explained,

> Researchers tell us there is a mechanism in our brain called the pleasure center. When activated by certain drugs or behaviors, it overpowers the part of our brain that governs our willpower, judgment, logic, and morality. This leads the addict to abandon what he or she knows is right. And when that happens, the hook is set and Lucifer takes control. ("O That Cunning Plan of the Evil One," *Liahona*, November 2010)

Why, then, are so many of us drug addicts content with standing on the sidelines instead of striving to make entrance into the game of life? This type of hiding becomes exhausting for addicts since their mind frame will always be filled with regret, sadness, self-pity, resentments, and discontent. Deep down, every addict wants to be competing in the game, whether they like to admit it or not. Standing on the sidelines means selfishness and laziness, which are attributes that are in the opposite direction of God. And the further that one gets away from God, then the closer they become to being of "the natural man [which] is an enemy to God" (Mosiah 3:19).

If we do choose to get into the game of recovery, we will most certainly get battered and bruised early on, but "all these things shall give thee experience, and shall be for thy good" (D&C 122:7). Addiction creates holes in our character, so we must fill these holes before we can ever become a coach ourselves. "Therefore, what manner of men ought ye to be? Verily I say unto you, even as I am" (3 Nephi 27:27).

The School of Addiction is not for the faint of heart. It demands hard work in order to pass. The School of Cancer, for instance, can lean upon medications and radiation for treatment. But no such thing happens in the School of Addiction since the treatment depends on Him "healing

[our] every sickness and every disease" (Matthew 9:35), and becomes a lifelong effort of enduring to the end (see 1 Nephi 22:31).

Mental toughness is what's needed in order to live a sober life. And we cannot get mentally tougher if we aren't willing to take a beating from time to time. After all, how are we ever going to learn to roll with the punches if we are always afraid of getting hit? "Be sober, be vigilant; because your adversary the devil, as a roaring lion, walketh about, seeking whom he may devour" (1 Peter 5:8).

Then you have those players who have gotten some playing time but are still just partially in the game. They changed a few things, but their character still has many holes in it due to them not working the twelve-step repentance process. Yes, they have some clean time, but soon enough they don't have some clean time. And back and forth this exhausting cycle goes until they are back on the sidelines full time again. These people watch in awe of those who are consistent players in the game but don't have the courage to be consistent themselves.

To have courage means to get uncomfortable, and the only way to get good at being uncomfortable is to lean on Christ for support. And Christ's support does not come to those who are not willing to support themselves first by seeking to abstain from those things in the world that are bad and addictive. It is only after we step on the field and take the Savior's yoke upon us that "we shall find rest unto our souls" (Matthew 11:29).

These same sideliners know all the recovery lingo, but lack the deep understanding of life's purpose that only comes to those that seek after Christ and His lifestyle of health. And since they are not active participators in the repentance process, they lack depth and are thus unable to change. Such people are found coaching on the sidelines and cannot reach their full potential as leaders since they are only talkers and not doers. After all, the best coaches are those who have suffered in the trenches alongside their troops. "For how knoweth a man the master whom he has not served, and who is a stranger unto him, and is far from the thoughts and intents of his heart?" (Mosiah 5: 13).

Others are playing in the game but are merely going through the motions. They are sober and are making progress, but are still selfish and end up living far below their potential due to their stoppage in seeking after Christ-like attributes. In this stage, many claim that their spiritual condition is high enough and that they are cured, but we are never cured. There will always be something to quit, and the moment we stop trying to quit something is when we lose everything. Remember, the twelve-step repentance process is a daily practice and not a one-time thing. Repentance is a way of life!

Numerous players are giving it their all in the game so as to capture the type of character that will enable them to become great in this life. These individuals are experiencing the abundant life because they have figured out how to deal with stress and pain by leaning on the Holy Spirit for support. Such players have found out the truth about Christ and His beautiful lifestyle since they have been active competitors on His strait and narrow path.

Many new players to the game fall victim to "[running] faster than [they have] strength" (Mosiah 4:27). The lights are so bright, and it's so exciting to finally be playing that they fail to take the necessary steps in between before they reach the end zone to "win the prize" (Mosiah 4:27). They want to hurry it all up; then they loose their footing, end up falling, and are soon back on the sidelines with the "poor me" attitude.

Therefore, as players in the game, we must "see that all these things are done in wisdom and order" (Mosiah 4:27) so that our focus can remain on those things that matter the most, like our family and spiritual work. We must keep our cool even when we feel like being hot. And we must get rid of those behaviors that aren't in line with the Spirit. Being loud in our behavior, talking behind people's backs, carrying resentments, and participating in too much of the entertainment hustle and bustle will lead us to having too much baggage. We must quiet our lives down so that we can hear the "still small voice" (1 Nephi 17:45).

Some players are always leaning on their parents for support during the game and by so doing are never granted the opportunity to achieve self-reliance. These parents may have been great players in the game themselves, even achieving Christ-like attributes, wealth, and stability; but their posterity has lacked the ability to put on a performance under the game time lights. Self-reliance must be achieved or no trophies will be granted at the end of the game.

THE TWO BELIEF SYSTEMS

It is true that there are better belief systems than others. Some try to believe in nothing; others try to believe in something. The one who tries to believe in blackness after death may have a hard time seeing any purpose in life. This earth and life were all a big mistake, right? I mean, what is the purpose of life if after we die there is nothing but blackness in the casket? And if there is no life after death, then there was no life before death either, right? And so are we all here on this earth to just have the best time possible before our hundred years is up? So should we seek happiness through the pleasure-filled lifestyle? What does it matter anyway if after we die there is no hope for a reuniting of body and spirit to live with our family members again?

Or we can try and believe that "the graves were opened; and many bodies of the saints which slept arose, And came out of the graves after his resurrection, and went into the holy city, and appeared unto many" (Matthew 27:52–53. See also 3 Nephi 23:9–11).

"O death, where is thy sting? O grave, where is thy victory? (1 Corinthians 15:55).

"O how great the plan of our God!" (2 Nephi 9:13).

Which is the more beautiful belief system to try and develop faith in? The blackness belief system? Or the life before and after death belief system—that "God himself that formed the earth . . . created it not in vain, he formed it to be inhabited" (Isaiah 45:18)?

Is it better to try and believe that we are all here by mistake and that after we die, we won't see our loved ones again? Or is it better to try and believe in a loving Creator who "is our God; and we are the people of his pasture, and the sheep of his hand" (Psalm 95:7), a God who has a plan for us and our family after we die?

Is it better to try and believe that this life has no purpose, so we should just live it up and experience pleasure to the fullest? Or is it better to try and believe that this life is a test and proving ground, "to see if [we] will do all things whatsoever the Lord [our] God shall command [us]" (Abraham 3:25), thus holding us accountable to God for the way that we act?

Yours is to choose which way to believe—but keep in mind that both belief systems take faith. And if you think about it, the one belief system takes an even greater amount of faith than the other, since it's linked to escaping accountability to a higher power for the way that we act in this life.

But being accountable to someone or something is what this life is all about, isn't it? Accountable to our wife and kids. Accountable to our boss. Accountable for following the laws of the land, and much more. This life is filled with accountability partners, and when we try and escape accountability is where we run into problems. Every human being has strong passions and desires, but that doesn't mean we should act out in the way that we feel. No wonder the world is headed south in a quick way, since the new religion has become pleasure seeking. No wonder the world is filled with gross sex crimes and pedophiles who commit horrific acts against innocent people. No wonder pornography is the new mind drug that is dragging people's hearts and souls through the gutter. No wonder drugs and alcohol are taking over people's lives and stealing their agency. No wonder the prisons are maxed out to full capacity. No wonder hundreds of thousands of people die every day from an overdose. No wonder!

LIFE IS A TEST

What is wrong with believing that life is a competition and test? What is wrong with believing that if we do our best to abstain from the world, then great will be our blessings in this life and the next? For some, it's far easier to believe that our performance in the School of Addiction doesn't matter since the Head Coach treats us all as equals no matter how we act. For me, that concept doesn't work. Why would I care to change and compete if God doesn't care if I change or compete? Many seek to believe that we just have to show up to class, and we will get an A. For me, I must believe that I have to compete with myself in this life, and to "ye therefore perfect, even as your Father which is in heaven is perfect" (Matthew 5:48). Obviously, we can never be perfect, but we can darn sure try.

For example, the philosophy of the coach should be to play his best players so long as they show up to practice, work hard in school, and do what they are told. We all know the one kid who does not work hard nor follow the coach's rules but has equal ability, if not more, than the kid who does what the coach asks. This boy will find himself not playing in the game on Friday night. Why should he be rewarded the opportunity to play when he has not sacrificed like the other players? Likewise, in the School of Addiction, who will be rewarded the opportunity of becoming a teacher and coach: the student who goes through the motions and doesn't do a whole lot, or the one who shows up to class and goes hard on the curriculum?

Isn't all of life like this? In our work and professional lives, we are required to follow rules and work hard. In many cases, the one who works hard gets promoted, and the one who doesn't gets fired. In the School of Addiction, we have to compete with ourselves if we want to make it through. We cannot believe that anything will be handed to us, because it won't. We must be competitors!

Now, I'm not telling you to stay trapped in shame and regret. I'm saying you should "come unto Jesus with broken hearts and contrite spirits" (Mormon 2:14) since these feelings mean you care to improve and are saddened because of your love for God. We must see God as our Father in Heaven and Coach who might get a little mad and disappointed at first, but after we "sought forgiveness, with real intent" (Moroni 6:8), He will encourage us to get back on track in school and try again. Wouldn't our own father do such a thing? I know my father would never give up on me, nor would I with my kids. This is how we need to look at God because we are going to fall short quite often. Christ forgave everybody with whom He made contact. He will always forgive us in the School of Addiction since "his hand is stretched out still" (2 Nephi 19:17), though we must keep trying.

God does love the drug addict who is striving to walk His twelve steps of repentance: "He doeth not anything save it be for the benefit of the world; for he loveth the world, even that he layeth down his own life that he may draw all men unto him. Wherefore, he commandeth none that they shall not partake of his salvation" (2 Nephi 26:24).

BECOMING CHILDLIKE

Maybe we are to become as a child again, "submissive, meek, humble, patient, full of love, willing to submit to all things which the Lord seeth fit to inflict upon him, even as a child doth submit to his father" (Mosiah 3:19). Not childish, but becoming childlike. As children we jumped, played, and even dealt with boredom far better than we do now as addicted adults. Addicted adults are far more childish than even the young child by how they lack the ability to enjoy the simple things in life. These adults are always looking for fun through the escape, and have since grown from an innocent child to being of "the natural man" (Mosiah 3:19).

So the challenge in this life seems to be keeping our spiritual condition high enough to feel high enough in order to stave off pleasure seeking. Life seems to be full of monotony and repetitious experiences that can lead one to doubt purpose. Others can experience failure and continual relapse, which then leads them to feeling that life is hopeless and has no meaning. These same people wonder how there can be a God since He doesn't answer their prayers and make things better right away. They want it all now, and without the sacrifice of having to live His lifestyle in order to receive blessings. These people want the pleasure-filled lifestyle but still expect God to be happy about it. They want God in their lives, but they don't want to quit taking themselves out of reality by way of substances and immoral behavior.

It makes sense, then, why the Savior and His prophets of old gave counsel concerning the danger of our being "choked with cares and riches and pleasures of this life" (Luke 8:14).

What about the mother who changed her life in the School of Addiction and now works three jobs to keep her household running but found the gospel of Jesus Christ in the process? When times get hard, she leans on the gospel and has found peace through being sober even though her life is somewhat chaotic. She can do this because she has softened her heart and allowed God to take on some of her burdens. Yes, the jobs, raising the kids, and financial struggles are hard, but she has her Heavenly Father by her side. She knows with a surety that if she remains patient and sober, then all will be well with her and her family. Addiction has now become a blessing in her life because it led her to finding the gospel of Jesus Christ and a new set of character attributes. This woman has become softened, and even childlike.

I've seen this happen, so I know it to be true. It's an amazing thing when people develop a faith in God. When they truly believe that He is trying to lead them out of the shadows and back into the light. Let go of your hardness, if you have any, and try to develop this type of faith, and watch your life take off. But remember, you are on God's timetable, not yours. You cannot rush answers to your prayers. You cannot rush your progress in the School of Addiction because it's a school of "one day at a time." It takes a steady pace and a constant pressure over a long period of time in order to make progress; not a bunch of pressure all at once, and then no pressure at all.

CONCLUSION

But it all starts with you leaving your hard self behind and becoming softened. And if you won't leave your old self behind and become a "new creature" in Christ (2 Corinthians 5:17), then you are not going to change. Maybe the bottom hasn't dropped low enough, but I'm here to tell you that it soon will. Hopefully, it doesn't lead you to jail or the grave. However, if you can look beyond yourself a bit and on down the road, then you might see the destruction that lay ahead. You might see how pawning your parents' belongings will lead them to heartache and pain. You might see how your mom lies awake at night crying and praying that you are okay and one day will change. You might see how you'll be in and out of jail for years on end with felonies on your record so that when you do get out of jail, there is no hope for a good job. You might see your life as a borderline homeless person whom no one can trust nor tolerate. If this person is you, do you dare to let the gospel of Jesus Christ help you to change? The great question is this: who do we want to be in this life? Do we want to be junkie students who hang out in the parking lot of the School of Addiction, or do we want to be in the classrooms, working the program so that one day we can become coaches and teachers to those other students who need our help in the School of Addiction?

The beauty of the school is that it can bring us to our knees, an act of humility at our lowest point. At this point, we will finally realize that God, the Eternal Father, and His Son, Jesus Christ, are the only ones who can snatch us out of the hell that we are in and put us back into the classroom of the School of Addiction. It happened to me, and were it not for addiction, I would never have found the gospel of Jesus Christ, nor myself. I'm thankful for my addiction because now I am never alone, and rarely do I fear anything except for relapse, of course. But I do feel that it is good to fear relapse because it keeps me on the balls of my feet during the game instead of resting on the heels of complacency.

Let's soften up and follow the Savior.

CLASS 3
HOPE

"Happy is he that hath the God of Jacob for his help, whose hope is in the Lord his God."

Psalm 146:5

The first time I felt hope was when I was standing in front of a large painting of Christ at Temple Square, and I got this feeling that He might be able to help me. It wasn't a lightening-bolt type of a feeling, but was a small yet "perfect brightness of hope" (2 Nephi 31:20).

Because so many people get blinded by the world's shiny objects, they are not able to see the Light of the World's message of hope. "And the light shineth in darkness; and the darkness comprehended it not" (John 1:5).

It's quite sad to witness a grown adult mope around and be caught in the net of self-pity and laziness. The course on finding hope is simple, yet so many reek of self-pity that it complicates the curriculum. "I can't do it" or "I'm so depressed" are phrases that commonly describe the hopeless individual.

HOPE INSIDE RECOVERY MEETINGS

Hope can be found inside Christ's emergency rooms of Alcoholics Anonymous (AA), Narcotics Anonymous (NA), and the Church of Jesus Christ's Addiction Recovery Program (ARP), since "they that be whole need not a physician, but they that are sick" (Matthew 9:12).

Go to your recovery meetings and church meetings! And don't act like you don't have time! Go to one every day if you need to. The purpose is not for your entertainment. Instead, you go to these meetings so that you are not tempted with "wine nor strong drink; and he shall be filled with the Holy Ghost" (Luke 1:15). There are others in attendance at these meetings who will be good examples to you by how they have worked the twelve-step repentance process and are now "reconciled unto him through the atonement of Christ" (Jacob 4:11). Don't be scared at these meetings; just sit and listen, for the Comforter "shall teach [you] the truth and the way whither [you] shall go" (D&C 79:2). These meetings will help you find comfort as you hear others express how they found hope, God, and sobriety.

BECOMING A COACH

The only way for us to experience a life of sobriety is by being involved in a life full of service, thus becoming coaches and teachers in the School of Addiction. When one is truly changed by Christ's gospel, they do feel the need to teach and persuade others what they have come to know for themselves. "And when ye shall receive these things, I would exhort you that ye would ask God, the Eternal Father, in the name of Christ, if these things are not true; and if ye shall ask with a sincere heart, with real intent, having faith in Christ, he will manifest the truth of it unto you, by the power of the Holy Ghost" (Moroni 10:4).

Such was the case with Alma, he being "a very wicked and an idolatrous man. And he was a man of many words, and did speak much flattery to the people; therefore he led many of the people to do after the manner of his iniquities" (Mosiah 27:8).

Alma was an addict who was wicked and idolatrous. This courageous man eventually captured a spiritual experience that told him that he must quit much and be born again so that he could become much. And once he quit his poor habits, he went on to become the greatest missionary and coach the world has ever known, being an instrument "in the hands of God in bringing many to the knowledge of the truth, yea, to the knowledge of their Redeemer" (Mosiah 27:36).

But Alma had to wade "through much tribulation, repenting nigh unto death" before the miracle could happen (Mosiah 27:28).

Likewise, when addicts have hit their rock bottom and begun to change their lives by way of using Christ's gospel, then like Alma, they become those who want to help others to change through that same spiritual system, even becoming missionaries themselves.

We, too, must quit much in order to become much. The more we quit in this life, then the more useful we are to God, thus becoming "instruments in the hands of God" (Mosiah 27:36).

HOPE FOUND IN HEALTHY PRACTICES

Putting a beautiful schedule of health together and then sticking to it with exactness is an important piece of the hope puzzle.

What about waking up in the morning and being excited to act differently? On this day, we can "pray continually, that ye may not be tempted above that which ye can bear, and thus be led by the Holy Spirit" (Alma 13:28).

The early morning hours seem to be our best chance to experience the peace of the Spirit. Some exercise, a good breakfast, then followed by some study from the scriptures, and finally, some prayer are practices that are built upon "the rock of our Redeemer, who is Christ, the Son of God" (Helaman 5:12). Such practices will lead us to feel safe:

When the devil shall send forth his mighty winds, yea, his shafts in the whirlwind, yea, when all his hail and his mighty storm shall beat upon you, it shall have no power over you to drag you down to the gulf of misery and endless wo, because of the rock upon which ye are built, which is a sure foundation, a foundation whereon if men build they cannot fall. (Helaman 5:12)

How comforting it is to know such sublime truths; that if we stay active participators in the gospel of Jesus Christ that no matter what "mighty storm shall beat upon you," we can take comfort in knowing that we are upon "a foundation whereon if men build they cannot fall" (Helaman 5:12).

Therefore, we can take great courage in knowing that we cannot fail in the game of life if we are "the humble followers of Christ" (2 Nephi 28:14).

Each day, we can work on being patient, avoid talking and thinking bad about others, watch what we say and think about, and carry a personality of reverence, charity, and meekness. Thus, being led by the Holy Spirit, we become "humble, meek, submissive, patient, full of love and all long-suffering" (Alma 13:28).

In order to feel all right in our heads, we must act all right out in the world. Imagine the peace that could be experienced if we could "search diligently in the light of Christ that ye may know good from evil"; and that if we "will lay hold upon every good thing, and condemn it not, ye certainly will be a child of Christ" (Moroni 7:19).

And finally, we cannot forget what practices got us to the point of feeling good about ourselves. We must hold true to the routine of exercise, good nutrition practices, scripture study, meeting attendance, and the constant effort to emulate the character of Christ. King Benjamin said, "I would that ye should remember, and always retain in remembrance, the greatness of God, and your own nothingness, and his goodness and long-suffering towards you" (Mosiah 4:11; see also Moses 1:9–10).

Remember, we have to stay competing with ourselves (obedient to the commandments), or we will get sick again with our addiction disease and become "past feeling" once again.

HOPE FOUND IN THE GOSPEL OF JESUS CHRIST

And when your day is hard, and you are caught up in dreadful thinking, then you can "be secure, because there is hope" (Job 11:18) that God will see you through it. On Sunday night when you are dreading the Monday morning workload, just "decide to turn your will and your life over to the care of God the Eternal Father and His Son, Jesus Christ" (see Addiction Recovery Program, "Step 3: Trust in God," https://addictionrecovery.lds.org/steps/3). And then when Monday finally passes, you will see how God helped you and that the day wasn't nearly as bad as you thought it was going to be.

The hope that is found in the gospel of Jesus Christ can help you to deal with dread, depression, and anxiety, and will lead you to live in a present and peaceful mind frame.

If we can practice remaining present in our minds, then there leaves little room for dread, worry, doubt, resentments, and, of course, cravings. Therefore, we should "look unto [the Lord] in every thought" (D&C 6:36).

The Lord has asked the question, "What manner of men ought ye to be?" And He answered, saying, "Even as I am" (3 Nephi 27:27). This tells us that Christ should always be on our minds so that we can "always have his spirit to be with [us]" (Moroni 4:3). And when our thoughts do drift in a poor direction, we can pull our minds back into the present "and pray always, lest ye be tempted by the devil" (3 Nephi 18:15).

At a family party, or around our wife and kids, we should always seek to be present so that we can appreciate those family moments that matter the most. Likewise, when studying, reading, and praying to God, we should strive to remain present so that our spiritual work can be more meaningful. And besides, if we are not present and focused during spiritual work, then it will not work.

Christ was also enrolled in the School of Addiction during His mortal ministry, and when He fasted in the desert for forty days. During this forty day fast, He was tempted three times, each of which He abstained from doing, even though "he was afterward an hungred."

And when the tempter came to him, he said, If thou be the Son of God, command that these stones be made bread.

But he answered and said, It is written, Man shall not live by bread alone, but by every word that proceedeth out of the mouth of God.

Then the devil taketh him up into the holy city, and setteth him on a pinnacle of the temple,

And saith unto him, If thou be the Son of God, cast thyself down: for it is written, He shall give his angels charge concerning thee: and in their hands they shall bear thee up, lest at any time thou dash thy foot against a stone.

Jesus said unto him, It is written again, Thou shalt not tempt the Lord thy God.

Again, the devil taketh him up into an exceeding high mountain, and sheweth him all the kingdoms of the world, and the glory of them;

And saith unto him, All these things will I give thee, if thou wilt fall down and worship me.

Then saith Jesus unto him, Get thee hence, Satan: for it is written, Thou shalt worship the Lord thy God, and him only shalt thou serve.

Then the devil leaveth him, and, behold, angels came and ministered unto him. (Matthew 4:3–11)

Christ must've had hope during His forty-day fast, and we can lean on His example of not giving in to temptation even when our physical self is weak. Paul counseled, "For in that he himself hath suffered being tempted, he is able to succour them that are tempted" (Hebrews 2:18). "For we have not an high priest which cannot be touched with the feeling of our infirmities; but was in all points tempted like as we are, yet without sin" (Hebrews 4:15. See also D&C 62:1).

Therefore, because of Christ's experience in the School of Addiction, He was given a perfect understanding of how to coach and empathize with us as we struggle with temptation. "Nevertheless the Son of God suffereth according to the flesh that he might take upon him the sins of his people, that he might blot out their transgressions according to the power of his deliverance" (Alma 7:13).

The physical sickness that comes from withdrawals, along with the dark mind struggles, is real. The depression that follows, coupled with feelings of hopelessness, is real. Christ felt our pain when He was upon the cross and in Gethsemane when He "fell on his face, and prayed, saying, O my Father, if it be possible, let this cup pass from me: nevertheless not as I will, but as thou wilt" (Matthew 26:39).

Therefore, we can lean on His love for us when we feel as if the temptation and suffering might be too much. It's not too much, and if we can get past the roadblock in our mind, then we will soon see that it is possible to remain sober in this life. Choose hope over fear. Choose light over dark. Choose right over wrong. And lastly, choose to lean upon the teachings of the gospel of Jesus Christ. After all, they are what make up the curriculum here in the School of Addiction.

NO COMPLAINING, MURMURING, OR RESENTING

In order to remain hopeful, we need to be cheerful and happy and not wasting time complaining or murmuring. Complaining, talking behind people's back, and feeling sorry for ourselves are not practices of individuals who carry hope; these are practices that lead to resentment, self-pity, and despair.

Neal A. Maxwell explained, "A basic cause of murmuring is that too many of us seem to expect that life will flow ever smoothly, featuring an unbroken chain of green lights with empty parking places just in front of our destinations" ("Murmur Not," *Ensign*, November 1989).

Resentments are those false narratives that are deeply rooted in the mind of an addict. They will twist our minds up to the point of us not being able to discern between what's real and what's fake. If we allow these resentments to travel too far, then we can start acting out in self-pity, murmuring, and even saying things to others that are hurtful and not appropriate. These thoughts will ruin our chance to feel the warmth of the Spirit, and if we can't feel the Spirit, we will not stay sober, even becoming "past feeling [having] given [ourselves] over unto lasciviousness, to work all uncleanness with greediness" (Ephesians 4:19).

When one is caught in a resentment attack, the mind becomes so bothered and irritated at the past or present acts of others that we start building out over-the-top scenarios and assumptions in our minds. This madness and contention for others leads us to being locked away in our heads. And when one is locked up, they almost always look for an escape route, either back through the worldly substances, or the better way—through God's grace that is "sufficient for the meek" (Ether 12:26).

So watch what gossip circles you are spending time in, and don't be a complainer and a comparer, which are practices that will feed the resentment mind frame. If you are constantly comparing yourself to others or are one who tries to get people on your side, then you will come home feeling hopeless and regretful, which is a mind frame that is not successful in the School of Addiction. "Moreover if thy brother shall trespass against thee, go and tell him his fault between thee and him alone: if he shall hear thee, thou hast gained thy brother" (Matthew 18:15).

Therefore, choose to stay positive even when others are trying to get you to gossip with them. This nongossip type of approach will free you from feeling self-conscious. And when that somebody who was being talked about is around, you won't have to worry if he or she knows what was being said behind their back since you chose to step outside of the gossip circle. Now hope has room to develop in your soul because the garbage has been taken out. "My peace I give unto you: not as the world giveth, give I unto you. Let not your heart be troubled, neither let it be afraid" (John 14:27).

Remember, competitiveness towards others, where we want them to fail so that we might have the opportunity to say "I told you so" isn't a good way to be. Our ultimate hope should be for thoughts of gratitude and helpfulness to be taking up space in our minds so that we can escape being "racked with eternal torment" (Alma 36:12).

COMPETE WITH OUR DEMONS

Prayer, scripture study, and jogging are three practices that can help us to straighten our mind frame out. Jogging in a beautiful setting while listening to good sounding music can lift our thoughts just enough to allow prayer and gratitude to develop. And then those thoughts of madness towards others and ourselves will be enveloped in "the pure love of Christ" (Moroni 7:47).

There have been many times when my mind has been filled with this madness and contention, but it wasn't until I had the courage to put my headphones on and go for a walk while listening to the Book of Mormon that I could finally see "things as they really are, and of things as they really will be" (Jacob 4:13).

You see, we get blinded by these resentment lights, and the great cure can be jogging, good sounding music that edifies, prayer, and finally "feasting upon the word of Christ" (2 Nephi 31:20).

Our minds seem to work best after exercise, which is why afterwards in our cool-down walk, we should take the opportunity to "pray unto the father in the name of Jesus" (3 Nephi 19:6); and then perhaps sit in the shade of a tree and "ponder the path of life" (Proverbs 5:6).

DON'T BE MOODY

Around our family members and close friends, our mood may be low, and our desire to be negative and isolated will be great, but we mustn't act like a child since this is a form of selfishness and self-pity that screams pathetic. We can expect our mood to be up and down since that is the tale of life. And just because we are in a bad mood does not mean we are having a bad day or are unhappy. It just means that we are in a bad mood, and it will soon pass. The more time we spend sober, then our mood will more frequently become stable and balanced. We can hope and pray for this stable mood! "Yea, humble yourselves, and continue in prayer unto him" (Alma 34:19).

Sometimes our moodiness means we have high expectations for ourselves, and when we fall short, we feel as if we let ourselves down. We cannot become victims of our moods just because we are in a constant search to improve our character. Remember, we have many character holes, especially early on in the school, so we cannot let our moods lead us into believing that we are unhappy and not making progress. And besides, the Lord's prophet has counseled us "that all these things are done in wisdom and order; for it is not requisite that a man should run faster than he has strength" (Mosiah 4:27).

During a baseball game, you have those players who perform poorly at the beginning of the game but end up finishing strong. They quickly forget about their failures in the first few innings. By contrast, there were other players who dwell on their poor performance in those first few innings, which causes them to perform poorly during the entire game. The point is, we must move on and not dwell on our past moods and performances. Stop worrying about those things that are totally out of your control and focus on those things that you can control—things like exercise, healthy eating, scripture study, church and meeting attendance, service, how you choose to view the world, how you react to adversity, and, of course, how you treat people, among many others.

CONCLUSION

Viktor Frankl, a man who experienced the evils of the Auschwitz concentration camp during World War II, carried a special hope and attitude that eventually carried him to freedom and peace. He would not allow his poor circumstances to affect his mood, which caused the guards and his fellow prisoners to experience hope themselves. His perfect brightness of hope made him untouchable, as was the case with Gandhi and many other great men and women who were perfectionists in the Class of Hope.

President David O. McKay said, "It is our duty to seek to acquire the art of being cheerful. It will hold in check the demons of despair and stifle the power of discouragement and hopelessness" (*Treasures of*

Life [Deseret Book, 1965]). Remember, we must meet God halfway, and then He will do the rest. When our days look dull and hopeless, if we will just stay sober, then we are making all the progress we need to be. Just stay "humble, meek, submissive, patient, full of love and all long-suffering" (Alma 13:28) and all will be well with you in the School of Addiction.

CLASS 4
HEALTH

"And shall find wisdom and great treasures of knowledge, even hidden treasures;

"And shall run and not be weary, and shall walk and not faint.

"And I, the Lord, give unto them a promise, that the destroying angel shall pass by them, as the children of Israel, and not slay them. Amen."

D&C 89:19–21

The person just out of jail or rehab is oftentimes scared and has no idea what he or she is going to do with their lives. They are a bit like the prodigal son who "took his journey into a far country, and there wasted his substance with riotous living" (Luke 15:13). And after one too many parties they ran out of "substances" to keep that party alive, in which they "began to be in want" (Luke 15:14) of a new way of life. So they traveled into the rooms of jail or rehab to be taught further in the School of Addiction. And when released back out into the world to try their hand at competing, they are newly humbled and "say unto him, Father, I have sinned against heaven, and before thee, And am no more worthy to be called thy son: make me as one of thy hired servants. And he arose, and came to his father. But when he was yet a great way off, his father saw him, and had compassion, and ran, and fell on his neck, and kissed him" (Luke 15:18–20).

REPLACE IT WITH THE GOSPEL OF JESUS CHRIST

For those of us who are trying to remain on the strait and narrow path, we should replace the dark hole that addiction left in us with the bright light of the gospel of Jesus Christ. The gospel of Jesus Christ is a beautiful program of health that will lead you to being changed in such a massive way that your addiction will eventually be looked upon as being a great blessing.

It's easy to get addicted to coming home and sitting on the couch to take the easy way out through the pill or drink. However, it's not as easy to come home and go to the gym, cook a healthy dinner, stay present around your family, read your scriptures, say your prayers, and go to bed early. The health of the gospel of Jesus Christ is far harder to get addicted to than a substance, but once it happens, it is the far better addiction. There is no other system of health on the planet Earth that can cause a person to become a "new creature" (2 Corinthians 5:17) like the gospel can.

How incredible would it be to never be alone and to be supported with our weaknesses at all times? "And if men come unto me I will show unto them their weakness. I give unto men weakness that they may be humble; and my grace is sufficient for all men that humble themselves before me; for if they humble themselves before me, and have faith in me, then will I make weak things become strong unto them" (Ether 12:27).

God will truly make "weak things become strong" if we will just become those who seek after His lifestyle of health. I've seen this miracle happen in my own life, and it's guaranteed to happen in your life as well if you will just compete to the best of your ability, since His "grace is sufficient for all men that humble themselves before me" (Ether 12:27).

I'll do whatever you want me to do, Heavenly Father. If you want me to start going to church and AA meetings, then I will. If you want me to start praying, then I'm cool with that as well. If you want me to lay low on the weekends and spend time with my family, well, then fine. I'm all in, Heavenly Father. Please help me change my life because I cannot do it alone. Please help me learn and live your lifestyle. I'm ready!

This is the type of attitude we need in order to get addicted to the health of Christ's gospel. We have to let God step in and replace our badness with His goodness.

CREATE NEW HEALTHY MEMORIES

First, we need to start being creative in order to deal with the cravings. We must create new memories that will outshine the bad memories. We can't be afraid to throw on our headphones and go jogging in a unique place that is full of scenery, where we switch back and forth from jogging listening to music, to then walking listening to conference talks or the scriptures. The combination of exercise, scenery, uplifting music, and the word of God will change our mind frame to one that is now full of gratitude, peace, and serenity.

"God grant me the serenity to accept the things I cannot change, courage to change the things I can, and wisdom to know the difference" (Alcoholic Anonymous).

We can't be afraid to go to the local high school track to run sprints, work on prayer, do some reading under the shade of a tree, and further "meditate upon these things" (1 Timothy 4:15), even thanking Heavenly Father for giving us the courage to make such an experience happen.

We can't be afraid to turn up the intensity of our experiences so that our angers and frustrations can be replaced by the discomfort of burning lungs, legs, and a highly elevated heart rate. We can't be afraid to reach the point of failure and exhaustion, because afterward we will be proud of ourselves for our intense efforts, and our dark mind will be replaced with "the mind of the Lord, that he may instruct [us]" (1 Corinthians 2:16).

Walking is important as well, since running and being intense aren't always appropriate. Going for a 60-minute walk while listening to the word of God and then uplifting music can do so much for our soul. Walking in quiet, beautiful places during the early morning or just before dark does something to our eyes and mind that is indescribable. Those moments are when we can find the most gratitude for scenery and the beautiful world we live in, which then will lead us to further gratitude for the gospel of Jesus Christ and our family. After all, walks with our families are a great form of spiritual work.

Christ, after feeding the five thousand, went on a walk and "departed again into a mountain himself alone" (John 6:15). Even the Son of God needed some time away from the multitudes of people to work on His relationship with His Father in Heaven. Likewise, we need to create walking experiences for ourselves in unique and beautiful places so that we, too, can work on our relationship with our Father in Heaven. And if we do these walks consistently, nostalgia can be very useful: "I would ask, can ye feel so now?" (Alma 5:26). By seeking after past spiritual experiences, one may develop a better understanding of what God is trying to do with them in the School of Addiction.

HEALTHY ENTERTAINMENT

What about learning to enjoy healthy entertainment? On the weekends, we can get excited about seeing a good movie in the theater or watching a good series or even sports. The idea is to learn how to get excited about entertainment in a healthy way without feeling the need to take something during the process.

Elder D. Todd Christofferson had this to say about healthy entertainment:

> Just as honest toil gives rest its sweetness, wholesome recreation is the friend and steadying companion of work. Music, literature, art, dance, drama, athletics—all can provide entertainment to enrich one's life and further consecrate it. At the same time, it hardly needs to be said that much of what passes for entertainment today is coarse, degrading, violent, mind-numbing, and time wasting. Ironically, it sometimes takes hard work to find wholesome leisure. When entertainment turns from virtue to vice, it becomes a destroyer of the consecrated life. "Wherefore, take heed . . . that ye do not judge

that which is evil to be of God." ("Reflections on a Consecrated Life," *Liahona*, November 2010)

Likewise, it is the same with our hobbies for mountain biking, skiing, or fishing. Many of these hobbies were tainted due to our past use of substances; however, it is totally possible to relive these hobbies by being clean and sober. We need to look at our hobbies as being a great form of spiritual work, and if we take ourselves out of reality while doing them, then we are driving the Spirit from out of our system.

In the words of Paul, "What? know ye not that your body is the temple of the Holy Ghost which is in you, which ye have of God, and ye are not your own? For ye are bought with a price: therefore glorify God in your body, and in your spirit, which are God's" (1 Corinthians 6:19–20).

President Ezra Taft Benson gave this beautiful description on health when he said,

> The condition of the physical body can affect the spirit. That's why the Lord gave us the Word of Wisdom. He also said that we should retire to our beds early and arise early (see D&C 88:124), that we should not run faster than we have strength (see D&C 10:4), and that we should use moderation in all good things. In general, the more food we eat in its natural state and the less it is refined without additives, the healthier it will be for us. Food can affect the mind, and deficiencies in certain elements in the body can promote mental depression. A good physical examination periodically is a safeguard and may spot problems that can be remedied. Rest and physical exercise are essential, and a walk in the fresh air can refresh the spirit. Wholesome recreation is part of our religion, and a change of pace is necessary, and even its anticipation can lift the spirit. ("Do Not Despair," *Ensign*, November 1974)

Therefore, we have to go out and find stuff to enjoy. How are we ever going to find out if we enjoy something if we do nothing? Be creative and create for yourself. Swim, bike, run, lift weights, go on walks, play sports, eat healthy, watch and go to movies, go fishing and skiing, and much more. Be creative! This is how you will switch paths from off the six-lane addiction freeway, to the "strait and narrow course" (Helaman 3:29).

SEEING OURSELVES IN A POSITIVE LIGHT

What about daydreaming while listening to good music? When Saul was battling with an evil spirit, "David took an harp, and played with his hand: so Saul was refreshed, and was well, and the evil spirit departed from him" (1 Samuel 16:23). When wrapped up in our drug of choice, we never could daydream about beautiful concepts or hear music. But as we clear up, we can hear music, and it can lead us to thinking beautifully. I always heard while growing up that we shouldn't be daydreaming as kids. And now, as an adult who struggles with addiction, I think it's wise to be daydreaming every so often. How important is it for us to finally see our own selves in a positive light? It is very important since addiction creates shameful, sad, and depressive thinking.

So yes, envisioning ourselves being a healthy and happy human being is a very important practice. Let music, exercise, and books lead you to seeing yourself in a positive light. Don't be afraid to go on drives or walks while listening to good music where you stop often to reflect, pray, read, daydream, and ponder. See yourself doing great things in the future, while also realizing that it's going to take one day at a time to get to that future. See yourself being happy with your family and one day having wealth and stability.

What about daydreaming of doing something great with your life? A business idea maybe, or thinking of a way you can help people in the School of Addiction to make progress. If you think about it, all this really involves is creating a vision of who you want to become in this life; and if we keep carrying this vision in our hearts and minds, then we will eventually make it happen. Thus, our motivation to stay sober will be great, since we will know that none of it will come true if we don't stay sober and work hard on the repentance process.

STATURE AND THE WEIGHT ROOM

Another healthy practice is participating in the weight room. The weight room will give you confidence by how it will change your stature. The definition of stature is the degree or development of a person: physically, mentally, morally, and spiritually.

The weight room will help you to achieve a new stature and toughness and will lead you to develop leadership qualities like the tough prophet Mormon: "[he] being young, was large in stature; therefore the people of Nephi appointed [him] that [he] should be their leader" (Mormon 2:1).

Mormon seemed to have carried a great character and physical presence, which tells us that he was athletic in body and strong in mind. We, too, should seek after a change in our stature and become like Mormon who was strong in mind, body, and spirit.

Nephi, another tough prophet, was also a man who was "large in stature . . . having received much strength of the Lord" and "having great desires to know of the mysteries of God" (1 Nephi 4:31; 1 Nephi 2:16). Nephi seemed to have carried a great physical presence and a desire know God, which tells us that he was an athletic man who sought revelation. We, too, should strive to elevate our character, physical presence, and our desire to know of the mysteries of God.

David defeated a lion, a bear, and finally the champion Goliath when he "took thence a stone, and slang it, and smote [Goliath] in his forehead, that the stone sunk into his forehead . . . and he fell upon his face to the earth" (1 Samuel 17:37, 49). Before the fight even began with Goliath, David had confidence in his physical and spiritual capabilities: "This day will the Lord deliver thee into mine hand; and I will smite thee, and take thine head from thee. . . . And all this assembly shall know that the Lord saveth not with sword and spear: for the battle is the Lord's, and he will give you into our hands" (1 Samuel 17:46–47).

To improve our strength and physical capabilities in an effort to become confident men and women who are "large in stature," we can learn to squat with a barbell on our back. I could write about a lot of weight room movements that could improve your physical stature, but the squat will do plenty since it is the most important lift. Starting Strength Coach and author Mark Rippetoe said,

> There is simply no other exercise, and certainly no machine, that produces the level of central nervous system activity, improved balance and coordination, skeletal loading and bone density enhancement, muscular stimulation and growth, connective tissue stress and strength, psychological demand and toughness, and overall systemic conditioning than the correctly performed full squat. (*Starting Strength: Basic Barbell Training* [Wichita Falls: Aasgaard Company, 2011])

Learn to squat, and learn to do it right! If you are doing this lift right, then you should be linear progressing each week and watching your loads increase along with your body and mind strength. After you learn to squat perfectly, then learn how to dead lift. Follow this with the press, clean, jerk, and finally the snatch.

The weight room takes discipline because it's not every day that we will be in the mood to go and train. Likewise, in life, we are hardly ever in the mood to go to work, school, or whatever, but we do it anyway, right? The weight room can teach us discipline because if we can be disciplined to it, then we can be disciplined to a lot of things. Being in the weight room teaches us how to get comfortable with being uncomfortable. Nothing in life is all that uncomfortable when compared to the gym experience. Therefore, the gym teaches us how to not fear anything in life. Stronger means better mentally, physically, spiritually, and even emotionally. After all, the stronger athlete is usually the better athlete. Likewise, the stronger soldier is usually the better soldier. And the one who struggles with addiction will be made stronger against their addiction disease if they stay close to the gym, and, of course, the gospel of Jesus Christ.

Rippetoe said it best:

If your expectations are always those of someone content to live without physical challenge, then when it comes time for mental, moral, or emotional challenge you fail to meet it because you are out of practice. Meeting and overcoming obstacles are skills that can be honed, as opposed to talents with which we are born. The best way to prepare for the inevitable shit that life occasionally hands us all is to live in a way that prepares you for it.If you can treat personal tragedy like a heavy set of 20 squats, you'll do better than someone who has never met any challenge. Intentionally placing yourself in the position of having to complete a task when you don't know if you can is the single best way of preparing to be in that position unintentionally. (*Strong Enough? Thoughts from Thirty Years of Barbell Training* [Wichita Falls: Aasgaard Company, 2007])

I have clients who suffer all day at their hard labor job but still find their way into the gym at night or in the early morning because they know how important it is for them to stay dialed into the barbell way of life. They have found that their sobriety depends on it. Therefore, no amount of fatigue can stop them from coming into the gym at night to pain train.

This is what I'm trying to teach you: never lean on the excuse that you are too busy or tired to go to the gym and train. The weight room is a gift from God to those of us who love to get high. We can get high in the weight room—so don't take it for granted. Replace it with the weight room! Replace it with the health of the gospel of Jesus Christ!

CONCLUSION

Remember, we need to feel good about ourselves if we are going to stay sober. It's important for us to be walking around in public liking how we look and feel. And if we don't like how we look and feel, then we won't like spending time in a sober mind frame. Don't be lazy! Put together a healthy routine and then stick to it! It is possible for you to get addicted to health since you are an addict. Think about it: if you can get addicted to drugs and alcohol, then you can also get addicted to the health of the gospel of Jesus Christ. However, if you want to experience the highs of our Heavenly Father, then you must be diligent in your pursuit of capturing them. "The soul of the sluggard desireth, and hath nothing: but the soul of the diligent shall be made fat" (Proverbs 13:4).

CLASS 5
LEARNING

"Seek ye diligently and teach one another words of wisdom; yea, seek ye out of the best books words of wisdom, seek learning even by study and also by faith."

D&C 109:7

There is no way to pass the School of Addiction without being a reader, studier, and writer. In the secular schools of today, we are required to be readers, studiers, and writers. It is the same in the School of Addiction.

In the gospel of Jesus Christ, there is quite the curriculum, and it will be up to you to learn it. President Boyd K. Packer said, "True doctrine, understood, changes attitudes and behavior. The study of the doctrines of the gospel will improve behavior quicker than a study of behavior will improve behavior. . . . That is why we stress so forcefully the study of the doctrines of the gospel" ("Little Children," *Ensign*, November 1986).

For me, I got into reading and writing when I was challenged to read and study about Christ by a group of female Mormon missionaries, and for them, I will forever be grateful. They led me to the Deseret Bookstore by Temple Square that had the course curriculum available to me, and that is where my study of Christ began. After studying for a few months and then discussing what I was reading with them, they challenged me to start keeping a journal, which continues to this day. My avid reading, studying, and journaling has led me to write about my own life experiences in the School of Addiction. Now my writing has turned into a small portion of the curriculum for the School of Addiction. Likewise, your writing can become a curriculum in the School of Addiction.

In *The Big Book* of Alcoholics Anonymous, we read stories about how people traveled from the depths of hell to finding peace and sobriety. These people created a curriculum in the School of Addiction that has helped many. We must write our story down so that others might be helped on down the road, like our children and future family members.

I've heard it said that there is nothing better than for our family members to be able to read our life story, even if it involves our rocky road in the School of Addiction. My children will read my books one day and will hopefully learn from my mistakes. Therefore, my walk in the School of Addiction will help them to pass their own courses in the school, whatever they may end up being.

A STUDY OF THE BOOK OF MORMON

First, become an avid reader of the scriptures. There is a difference between reading fiction and the self-help books of the gospel. I'm not saying get rid of Harry Potter, but have something from the gospel nearby, and read that the most, with little TV and no social media.

Bruce R. McConkie explained,

There are certain blessings that attend the study of the scriptures which are denied those whose studies and interests are in different fields. It is the study of the scriptures that enables men to gain revelations for themselves. Those who read the Book of Mormon, in the way Moroni specifies, gain a testimony of its truth and divinity, of the divine sonship of Christ, and of the prophetic call of Joseph Smith ("Come: Hear the Voice of the Lord," *Ensign*, December 1985)

I began a careful study of the Book of Mormon, and it helped me to change my behavior. I needed my spiritual condition to remain high in order to stay sober, and I found that if I stayed consistent with my reading from the Book of Mormon, I could experience further peace and safety. In my recovery, I have been one who has struggled intensely with cravings and even relapse. I found that when I am caught in the struggle of dark thinking, the Book of Mormon has the ability to feed some light into my mind.

Joseph Smith said that the Book of Mormon "was the most correct of any book on earth, . . . and a man would get nearer to God by abiding by its precepts, than by any other book" (*History of the Church*, 4:461). Well, I have participated in the Book of Mormon experiment and found out that what Joseph said was true. The book is correct and has brought me closer to God. The principles and concepts discussed in the Book of Mormon can only be captured if a careful, not casual, study takes place.

Moroni, a prophet in the Book of Mormon, makes this bold declaration:

> Behold, I would exhort you that when ye shall read these things, if it be wisdom in God that ye should read them, that ye would remember how merciful the Lord hath been unto the children of men, from the creation of Adam even down until the time that ye shall receive these things, and ponder it in your hearts.
>
> And when ye shall receive these things, I would exhort you that ye would ask God, the Eternal Father, in the name of Christ, if these things are not true; and if ye shall ask with a sincere heart, with real intent, having faith in Christ, he will manifest the truth of it unto you, by the power of the Holy Ghost.
>
> And by the power of the Holy Ghost ye may know the truth of all things. (Moroni 10:3–5)

WE MUST QUIT MUCH IN ORDER TO BECOME MUCH

I have become so grateful for the Book of Mormon because I can constantly lean on it for spiritual support. Inside the book, there are many stories of people who have transformed their lives by living the gospel, which gave me great hope that I, too, could change my own life.

We read of how Alma and the sons of Mosiah were addicts who were "wicked and . . . idolatrous" (Mosiah 27:8). These men eventually captured a spiritual experience that told them that they must quit much in order to become much. And once they quit their poor habits, they went on to become the greatest missionaries the world has ever known. "For they did publish peace; they did publish good tidings of good; and they did declare unto the people that the Lord reigneth" (Mosiah 27:37).

I gained from the example of these men—and there are others—that I must quit much in order to become much. And that the more I quit in this life, then the more useful I will be to God. I, too, want to be a great missionary and coach in this life, and so should you. Everyone should want to be a coach and great teacher, whether it's in your family, career, on in your calling at church. However, the only way to become a great teacher and coach is to be living the commandments of Christ so that the Holy Ghost can tell us "all things what [we] should do" (2 Nephi 32:3, 5).

Such insight about teaching and coaching was given to me as I carefully studied the Book of Mormon, for that is the power that lies within this special book. For those of you that are struggling with drug and alcohol addiction, this book has the power to change your behavior like it did mine. You will feel different if you are consistently studying this book. And that different feeling will make you take a hard look at how you are acting so that you don't drive that feeling away.

I noticed when I started studying the Book of Mormon that I was now watching my language, paying attention to what I watched on TV, what music I was listening to, and so on and so forth. Point being is that it heightened my spiritual condition to a level that felt amazing. But when I offended the teachings in that book, my spiritual condition then lowered, which caused me to feel uncomfortable and not as safe. If I spoke loudly and with vulgarity, I now noticed the change in my spiritual condition. If I watched something that was inappropriate, I then felt dark and uncomfortable.

We all know right from wrong because "that which is of God inviteth and enticeth to do good continually" (Moroni 7:13), but when we are wrapped up in our addictions, we become "past feeling" and confused (Moroni 9:20). However, when we start putting the Book of Mormon into our system, the "Light of Christ" makes its way back into our soul and helps us to discern between good and bad, so that we "do not judge wrongfully" (Moroni 7:18). And when we choose wrong, we can feel the Holy Ghost leave us, since "the Spirit of the Lord doth not dwell in unholy temples" (Helaman 4:24). Then we will want to choose right more often than the wrong so that we can remain feeling safe and at peace. The Savior promised, "Peace I leave with you, my peace I give unto you: not as the world giveth, give I unto you" (John 14:27).

The careful study of the Book of Mormon will feed a brand new knowledge and insight into your mind and heart on how to experience living the abundant life. And with knowledge comes power, responsibility, and finally accountability.

ACCOUNTABILITY PARTNER

I needed to be accountable for the way I was acting, and the Book of Mormon did such a thing. It taught me that if I wanted to experience peace and safety in this life, that I must seek with all of my heart, might, mind, and strength to live the commandments of Christ. "If ye love me, keep my commandments" (John 14:15).

All people that struggle with addiction need an accountability partner, and what better partner to have than Jesus Christ. A lot of people are scared to be held accountable for fear of having to feel bad about the way that they acted. They claim they feel too guilty, and so they go in search of an accountability partner that won't hold them to living such strict commandments.

President Boyd K. Packer explained it perfectly:

In mortality men are free to choose, and each choice begets a consequence. The choice Adam made energized the law of justice, which required that the penalty for disobedience would be death. But those words spoken at the trial, "Thou couldest have no power at all against me, except it were given thee from above" (John 19:11), proved mercy was of equal rank. A redeemer was sent to pay the debt and set men free. That was the plan.

Alma's son Corianton thought it unfair that penalties must follow sin, that there need be punishment. In a profound lesson Alma taught the plan of redemption to his son, and so to us.

Alma spoke of the Atonement and said, "Now, repentance could not come unto men except there were a punishment" (Alma 42:16).

If punishment is the price repentance asks, it comes at bargain price. Consequences, even painful ones, protect us. So simple a thing as a child's cry of pain when his finger touches fire can teach us that. Except for the pain, the child might be consumed.

I readily confess that I would find no peace, neither happiness nor safety, in a world without repentance. I do not know what I should do if there were no way for me to erase my mistakes. The agony would be more than I could bear. It may be otherwise with you, but not with me. ("Atonement, Agency, Accountability," *Ensign*, May 1988)

The thing that I'm learning the most from my study in the Book of Mormon is that Christ is determined to help us become the best version of ourselves in this life. And where we fall short, He will make up the difference so long as we tried our best, since His "grace is sufficient" (2 Corinthians 12:9). I learned that in order for me to become healed by the Atonement, then it must become a living and breathing thing in my life that I use daily, since I will fall short daily. Yes, I feel contrite and mad at myself quite often, but that does not discourage me, because life is a marathon and not a sprint. I know that if I keep learning from my mistakes and am always active in the repentance process, then one day I will become the best version of myself, even like Christ. I take comfort in knowing that "my strength is made perfect in weakness. Most gladly therefore will I rather glory in my infirmities, that the power of Christ may rest upon me" (2 Corinthians 12:9).

The challenges and trials that we all experience in life can be softened by the Spirit; and the Spirit can be obtained more significantly if we are constantly studying from the Book of Mormon. Early on, I seemed to be up and down in my mood and oftentimes felt little hope. However, the understanding that the Book of Mormon gave me concerning the plan of happiness led me to feeling hopeful. There were times in my recovery where I never thought I was going to be happy, and the Book of Mormon spoke to me "the truth of all things" (Moroni 10:5), helping me to feel "the Comforter" (D&C 79:2).

A BOOK OF CHARITY

I started creating scripture study experiences for myself in remote locations. I would drive up to a remote lake, or park at quiet cemeteries so that I could read in reverent solitude. Or I would go on a walk or hike while listening to the Book of Mormon from off my phone, which then would lead me to thoughts of charity. And I almost always found myself sending out healthy text messages, or making healthy phone calls to people I had not spoken to in a while. I found that this book carried a power in it that led me to a charitable mind frame "and a love of God and of all men" (2 Nephi 31:20). The more time I spent in it, the more I wanted to help people. I found myself looking past myself more frequently and on to others. Peter tells us that "above all things have fervent charity among yourselves; for charity preventeth a multitude of sins" (JST, 1 Peter 4:8), even relapse.

My kids often witness me study the Book of Mormon, and I almost always express to them how it has changed my life and that it's my most favorite book. Inside our home, it seems to be more reverent since bringing the Book of Mormon into it. The Book has led us to hang pictures of Christ on our wall, which has led to further peace and comfort inside our home. Remember Joseph Smith's promise that the "Book of Mormon was the most correct of any book on earth, . . . and a man would get nearer to

God by abiding by its precepts, than by any other book" (History of the Church, 4:461), which is why our home is now filled with the spirit since trying to "act in [its] doctrine" (D&C 101:78).

It's safe to say that the Book of Mormon has changed my life. It gave me hope when I had none. It provided me with a way to learn about the character of Jesus Christ so that I could go on to emulate His character. I love the way of life that Christ promoted people to live, and I will do my best moving forward to "be . . . therefore perfect" (Matthew 5:48).

If you are one who struggles with addiction and seems to be at the bottom, well then, what do you have to lose by reading the Book of Mormon? I used to go into the jails and prisons to present my concepts to the inmates. I loved doing this because in there I was speaking to a group of people who were at an all-time low. I would pitch the Book of Mormon to them like I am in this book, and they would eat it up because they were "powerless." I would tell them how the Book was changing my life and that I was sure it would do the same for them if they would begin a careful study of it.

I would have never read the Book of Mormon were it not for the experience of me being powerless to my addiction. But due to me being powerless and scared, I was open to hearing the gospel of Jesus Christ. To this day, I consider my addiction as a blessing, because there is no greater gift, in my humble opinion, than being a part of the cause of Christ; and I would have never made "entrance . . . into the everlasting kingdom of our Lord and Saviour Jesus Christ" (2 Peter 1:11) had I not become a drug addict first.

BE CREATIVE READERS, WRITERS, AND STUDIERS

We should therefore have books in our cars and on our phones so that we can make our downtime into reading time. Waiting in line for lunch or at the bank is a good time to read from off our smartphone; after all, you will gain more from an ebook than you will from Facebook. If we have thirty minutes to kill, then we can sit in our car and read our books. Reading eliminates boredom and gives us something to work on that can help us feel better about ourselves. A slow Saturday afternoon can now be transformed into a reading afternoon where we tie it in with jogging or hiking. We can jog a little while listening to an audiobook and then stop at a park along the way to read and pray. We may go on a drive to listen to music, but then stop in someplace quiet to get a reading experience in. These are a few of the many ideas of how you can read, but what I'm mostly promoting is that you become a creative reader, writer, and studier.

If you think about today's world and those who have found great success in business or leadership, I would dare to say that these men and women are readers and studiers. It was said that Abraham Lincoln used to read the same powerful book over and over until he knew the content better than the author. Great leaders make time for reading because they look at it as being a part of their job and career. In the School of Addiction, we must look at reading, studying, and writing as being our job since there is no way of passing if we are not studying the curriculum and writing the papers. "Wherefore, I said unto you, feast upon the words of Christ; for behold, the words of Christ will tell you all things what ye should do" (2 Nephi 32:3).

President Thomas S. Monson said,

Reading is one of the true pleasures of life. In our age of mass culture, when so much that we encounter is abridged, adapted, adulterated, shredded and boiled down, and commercialism's loudspeakers are incessantly braying, it is mind-easing and mind-inspiring to sit down privately with a good book. It is ennobling when that book contains the revealed word of God. ("Constant Truths in Changing Times," BYU Commencement, May 26, 1967)

"Seek ye out of the best books words of wisdom; seek learning, even by study and also by faith" (D&C 88:118).

Remember, becoming a reader, writer, and studier has to take place in the School of Addiction, or you will not pass the course. Just like you wouldn't pass a college course if you didn't study and turn in your papers. Treat it the same!

BECOMING A WRITER

To become a writer, try journaling about your experiences in the School of Addiction. Write about your jogging and spiritual experiences and how they made you feel. Write about your nutrition practices, or what you learned in your addiction recovery and church meetings. You can write about that craving you may have had and the darkness that you felt, followed by the light of overcoming. Don't worry about punctuation or grammar; just get it out. All of my writing has been on my phone. In this way, I can travel into solitude, and it is there where my mind seems to work best, especially after hiking or jogging in scenery, and in an intense way. Spencer W. Kimball described the process of inspired writing: "Those who keep a book of remembrance are more likely to keep the Lord in remembrance in their daily lives. Journals are a way of counting our blessings and of leaving an inventory of these blessings for our posterity" ("Listen to the Prophets," *Ensign*, May 1978).

CONCLUSION

We need to become intelligent and sharp! We have to be if we are going to be coaches who are always giving advice. A coach is a confident person, and it will be hard to find confidence if we do not believe what we are saying, which is why we must study. The student in college who prepares for his presentation to the class feels more confident than the student who did not prepare. Likewise, if we are going to become great coaches and missionaries, we sure better know the curriculum we are teaching or we will stop being called upon to coach and teach.

"And the Spirit shall be given unto you by the prayer of faith; and if ye receive not the Spirit ye shall not teach" (D&C 42:14).

"Now I need not rehearse the matter; what I have said may suffice. Behold, the scriptures are before you; if ye will wrest them it shall be to your own destruction" (Alma 13:20).

Alma and the Sons of Mosiah changed their lives. The scriptures tell us,

> And they traveled throughout all the land of Zarahemla, and among all the people who were under the reign of king Mosiah, zealously striving to repair all the injuries which they had done to the church, confessing all their sins, and publishing all the things which they had seen, and explaining the prophecies and the scriptures to all who desired to hear them.
>
> And thus they were instruments in the hands of God in bringing many to the knowledge of the truth, yea, to the knowledge of their Redeemer.
>
> And how blessed are they! For they did publish peace; they did publish good tidings of good; and they did declare unto the people that the Lord reigneth. (Mosiah 27:35–37)

Be one who "[feasts] upon the words of Christ" (2 Nephi 32:3). Be passionate about becoming a coach and missionary like Alma and the Sons of Mosiah. Remember, if you invest in yourself, then God will invest in you. He will send you people to work with since you are competent and prepared. This is a true story, and is currently happening to me. You could do it, too. Choose to become a reader, a writer, and a studier, so that you can become a good coach in the School of Addiction. There are a lot of people who need help. Let's be those people who can help. Learn and live the gospel of Jesus Christ.

CLASS 6
COMMUNICATION

"For when a man speaketh by the power of the Holy Ghost the power of the Holy Ghost carrieth it unto the hearts of the children of men."

2 Nephi 33:1

Isn't it interesting how often we brush off opportunities to communicate with others? What about the times when we might be able to share a good conversation with our dad or grandfather, but we don't because we are too caught up in our own selfish ways? Or when we are out running around looking to pick up drugs while our wife and kids are at home? They are wishing we were there so that we could be involved with them and could communicate to them how much we love and care for them. But we are not there because our love for the world and its shiny objects is pulling us away from them. How sad.

For the first three years of my children's lives, I was high and lost in the runaround. My wife kept our family intact and was mature when I was off acting like a selfish child. It was all about me, and never once did I care how my actions were affecting her. My communication was minimal, and most of the time the things I said were based on self-pity.

It was all about me during this time, until one day she had had enough and told me she was tired of me always talking about me. She asked me if I ever thought about her and the kids, which made me realize that I rarely asked about them. It was all about me, and only me. What a joke I was. I soon realized that this wasn't how my father raised me. I was not going be that way to my children and wife.

MY LITTLE GIRL AND GOD

The hard truth of it all for me is that I have never really liked spending time in reality until just recently, where my vision concerning life has now changed due to living the gospel of Jesus Christ. There was a time when I was letting my family down often, where I was always escaping into the land of amphetamine and opiate. Such a combination could never allow me to be myself, since my mood was either high or really low, which led me to irritability and depressive thinking. Taking my kids with me to meet my drug dealer at random spots. Driving with my kids in my car while being high on opiate. I'm so sad that this was who I was for a long time; I didn't even realize what I was doing, and that the example I was being for my kids was wrong—until one day as I was stopped at a stop light, high on opiate with my little girl in the back seat, that something finally wounded me deeply about the way of life that I was living, and that the example I was being for my little girl was wrong. I had just got done meeting my drug dealer at Barnes and Noble to pick up more methadone pills, when I looked back at my little girl while stopped at that red light, and she was looking at me with the most disappointed look that a three-year-old little girl could ever give her father. It was a look of disappointment that cut me so deep that I automatically started to cry. During that moment, I finally was able to see clearly that what I was doing was wrong, and that if I kept it up, I was going to lose my family. I saw how my little girl was never going to know who I truly was if I kept this sort of lifestyle up. I then looked back at her during that moment of when I was crying, and while she sat quietly in her car seat, and told her that I was sorry for letting her down so far in her life, and I promised to change.

I believe this is what has changed me, and is still changing me. It is true that "little children do have words given unto them many times, which confound the wise and the learned" (Alma 32:23). Instead of me searching for those pills in my pocket, I am now searching for a charitable character, which is a character I know cannot be developed through the participation in the worldly escape. I know that the worldly escape cannot provide me with the high that the spiritual gift of charity can provide me with. Therefore, my motivation to stay sober is great.

I'm so thankful for that short, quick, and tender experience that I shared with my little girl and God on that day. I'm thankful that I was able to hear what they said to me, even though there were no words said. Sometimes I think the greatest way for us to listen is through our hearts, for it's through our hearts that emotions can be found that pierce our soul deeply, then helping us to realize that we can be better than we are being. The room for improvement for the addicts' soul is great; but as our soul expands, then so will our vision concerning the big picture of life, which will help us to appreciate the small, simple moments that lay within our families—since we will have remained clear enough to notice. We will now be carrying a clarity and spiritual poise about us that will give way to a delightful character—one that will lead us to become an example of how to act and be in this life.

If you are one that is struggling with finding your way, just know that an eye-opening experience awaits you—only you must listen with your heart and not your ears. Don't be afraid to search for experiences that may cause you to cry, because it is through emotions such as these that you will take a deeper look at who you are and who you want to become.

How do you want to be remembered in this life? How do you want your children growing up? How do you want them to think about you? I know I want my children to always think of me as being their hero; the dad who fought the good fight in life and who did so confidently and without escape. I want them to remember how hard I have worked for them in hopes of providing them with a life that is filled with endless opportunities, where they can feel safe and comfortable because they will know that their dad is there to protect them from the storms of life, since he will have remained clear and free from all of the world's harmful, addictive substances, and will have remained physically and mentally strong, having a sound relationship with God, and will have taught his children how to be true disciples by giving them the understanding that God's ways are the great ways, and that true lasting happiness can only be obtained if they strive to "walk in the light of the Lord" (Isaiah 2:5)..

BE HONEST AND A GOOD LISTENER

Oh, how addiction affects how we communicate with others. When we are clear and living the healthy gospel of Jesus Christ, we are patient, kind, and reading and saying prayers with our children before bed. We don't take them for granted! However, when we are not clear, but full of the "natural man" (Mosiah 3:19), we are stuck in hurry-up mode where we don't take the time to communicate with our children because we are in a hurry to go back to being selfish. We essentially become liars and manipulators.

So you can start by being honest. Tell the truth about everything. When you feel yourself starting to lie or fib, then reverse yourself and tell the truth or just be quiet. We must learn when to be quiet instead of always trying to be heard. "Therefore, cease from all your light speeches" (D&C 88:121).

Remember, we are meek, humble, and submissive, so our personality is not one that should scream "Look at me." We need to listen intently as we let others talk so that when they are done, we can know what to say next "as the Spirit [gives us] utterance" (Acts 2:4). These people may need advice or counsel, and if we are not truly listening, but are only thinking about what it is that we want to say next, then we will miss our opportunity to be a coach and missionary. We must try and listen to people the entire time and refrain from cutting them off.

We have all been around that guy who has a better story to tell than everyone else; such a person is called a topper because he tops everyone else's story. We cannot be toppers in the School of Addiction because topping isn't consistent with being meek. And we need to remain meek people so that we can "delight [ourselves] in the abundance of peace" (Psalm 37:11).

Like Alma, we can let other people have the glory even when we might have something to say that would bring the glory on us. "I know that which the Lord hath commanded me, and I glory in it. I do not glory of myself, but I glory in that which the Lord hath commanded me; yea, and this is my glory, that perhaps I may be an instrument in the hands of God to bring some soul to repentance; and this is my joy" (Alma 29:9).

LEARN TO SHARE OUR STORIES

Another great way of communicating is to be open and learn to share your story. When talking to someone, you will open the door to sharing your story, and then they will feel comfortable with sharing who they are because of how you expressed to them that you have imperfections. Since no one is perfect, and everyone is fighting some sort of battle, then the communication will become two-way since you will both have shared in a common battle.

Alma was open and willing to communicate his addiction and conversion story to his son Helaman, which must have been a great experience for both father and son. In Alma's words,

> For I went about with the sons of Mosiah, seeking to destroy the church of God; but behold, God sent his holy angel to stop us by the way.
> And behold, he spake unto us, as it were the voice of thunder, and the whole earth did tremble beneath our feet; and we all fell to the earth, for the fear of the Lord came upon us.
> But behold, the voice said unto me: Arise. And I arose and stood up, and beheld the angel.

And he said unto me: If thou wilt of thyself be destroyed, seek no more to destroy the church of God.

And it came to pass that I fell to the earth; and it was for the space of three days and three nights that I could not open my mouth, neither had I the use of my limbs.

And the angel spake more things unto me, which were heard by my brethren, but I did not hear them; for when I heard the words— If thou wilt be destroyed of thyself, seek no more to destroy the church of God—I was struck with such great fear and amazement lest perhaps I should be destroyed, that I fell to the earth and I did hear no more.

But I was racked with eternal torment, for my soul was harrowed up to the greatest degree and racked with all my sins.

Yea, I did remember all my sins and iniquities, for which I was tormented with the pains of hell; yea, I saw that I had rebelled against my God, and that I had not kept his holy commandments.

Yea, and I had murdered many of his children, or rather led them away unto destruction; yea, and in fine so great had been my iniquities, that the very thought of coming into the presence of my God did rack my soul with inexpressible horror.

Oh, thought I, that I could be banished and become extinct both soul and body, that I might not be brought to stand in the presence of my God, to be judged of my deeds.

And now, for three days and for three nights was I racked, even with the pains of a damned soul.

And it came to pass that as I was thus racked with torment, while I was harrowed up by the memory of my many sins, behold, I remembered also to have heard my father prophesy unto the people concerning the coming of one Jesus Christ, a Son of God, to atone for the sins of the world.

Now, as my mind caught hold upon this thought, I cried within my heart: O Jesus, thou Son of God, have mercy on me, who am in the gall of bitterness, and am encircled about by the everlasting chains of death.

And now, behold, when I thought this, I could remember my pains no more; yea, I was harrowed up by the memory of my sins no more.

And oh, what joy, and what marvelous light I did behold; yea, my soul was filled with joy as exceeding as was my pain!

Yea, I say unto you, my son, that there could be nothing so exquisite and so bitter as were my pains. Yea, and again I say unto you, my son, that on the other hand, there can be nothing so exquisite and sweet as was my joy.

Yea, methought I saw, even as our father Lehi saw, God sitting upon his throne, surrounded with numberless concourses of angels, in the attitude of singing and praising their God; yea, and my soul did long to be there.

But behold, my limbs did receive their strength again, and I stood upon my feet, and did manifest unto the people that I had been born of God.

Yea, and from that time even until now, I have labored without ceasing, that I might bring souls unto repentance; that I might bring them to taste of the exceeding joy of which I did taste; that they might also be born of God, and be filled with the Holy Ghost. (Alma 36:6–24)

Alma is a great example of how to be honest. The tough prophet had no problem sharing his inspiring story because he had changed his life in a massive way. It seems likely that during this time of Alma sharing his story with his son Helaman that he would've shared his story with hundreds of people during his work as a prophet missionary. And the reason for Alma being such a good missionary was probably because of his past enrollment in the School of Addiction. The sinners would listen to Alma because he was once a sinner himself. It will be the same with us, but we must change our lives in the same way that Alma changed his life. We must capture a spiritual experience so that we can be "born again" (John 3:3).

COMMUNICATION AND SPIRITUAL CONDITION

It is in those circle meetings (ARP, AA, NA) that we, like Alma, can learn how to tell our story so that we can help others. In these addiction recovery meetings, we will learn how to talk in front of people, which is something that will be necessary for when we finally make it to becoming coaches in the School of Addiction. At first, it will be challenging and scary, but as time moves on, God will help you to speak so that others might be helped through your words. Addiction is a spiritual disease; and as we clear up and become more spiritual, our speech will become more fluent and concise, especially if we have been "feasting upon the words of Christ" (2 Nephi 31:20).

Our communication is dependent on our spiritual condition and vice versa. How we talk and what we choose to discuss and think about all play a role in our spiritual condition. If we are up late watching pornography, the next day our brain will be flooded with insecurities and doubt due to us not being able to feel any of the spirit in our system. Those images will make our communication efforts poor because they will flash in our mind, making it seem as if human relationships are nothing more than sexual. There is nothing worse than a mind that is constantly in the gutter of pornography. Such a mind frame cannot lead to great communication because no love can come from it. A trashy mind leads to trashy talk, and trashy talk isn't worth hearing about.

We will become great communicators if we "let all [our] things be done with charity" (1 Corinthians 16:14). Charity is a way of life and is "kind, and envieth not, and is not puffed up, seeketh not her own, is not easily provoked, thinketh no evil, and rejoiceth not in iniquity" (Moroni 7:45). Charity is having the "pure love of Christ" running through our system, "and whoso is found possessed of it at the last day, it shall be well with him" (Moroni 7:47).

If, however, we are constantly participating in immoral acts, then we cannot have this gift dwelling within us, which means our communication efforts will remain mediocre at best. "If ye have not charity, ye are nothing, for charity never faileth" (Moroni 7:46).

We cannot think that it's merely enough to get off of a particular substance when that substance is probably linked to immoral behavior. Our inhibitions lower when we are getting high or drunk, which then makes it far easier to participate in immoral behavior and vice versa. For example, the pills, the girls/guys, the drinks, the smokes, and the loud laughing and partying eventually all come to a quick halt when one finally loses everything. It's all linked, and if you want to escape the grips of drug and alcohol addiction and really learn how to communicate in an effective way, then you must make a determined effort to fix your flaws with being immoral as well. You have to learn how to communicate and socialize being sober and clear minded, and that's all there is to it.

TIME MANAGEMENT

There are also those times when we participate in hurried handshakes and rushed conversations. Someone may stop us in a hallway to talk and see how we are doing, but we hurry up and make it short, causing the person to feel as if he isn't important or worth our time. We need to stop and talk to people, even when we may not feel like talking. Who knows? These people might need someone to talk to about their struggles. And if we are good listeners, we will know what to say to them. Later, we will be thankful that we took the time to communicate with someone instead of hurrying past him. This happens all too often in our family relationships, and it's a sad thing when we start realizing that we've hurried past our parents and grandparents these past years without ever taking notice that they aren't going to live forever. Nothing lasts, so we should stop being selfish with our time. Time management is crucial in the School of Addiction.

Poor time management often happens when our mind is tied in the knot of contention and stress. It's hard to share a meaningful conversation with someone when our thoughts are mean.

We need to work on being present and not caught up in the future and past. For example, we cannot be moody with those that we love just because we may dread the following day's work schedule. For me, I usually start dreading Monday on Sunday night. Automatically, my lousy mood can be felt by my wife and kids. Nowadays, I'm staying focused on being present on Sunday night so that there will be no room for dread. If I'm present, I should not be thinking about Monday since I'm living in the moment with my family; and I'm giving them all of my time and positive energy instead of being a moody jerk.

COMMUNICATE WITH GOD

As a father, we can share our time with God by communicating to Him in prayer on behalf of our wayward son. Should our son end up in jail, he can use this time to clear up, be safe, and decide to read the scriptures since he will soon realize he has hit the bottom. These scriptures and brief time of clarity while in jail will give him a new perspective, and when it's time to leave the concrete walls behind, he will be better prepared than ever before to meet the challenges that lay ahead. The communication to God by the father for his wayward son was, in fact, an answer to his prayers even though the consequences of jail were harsh. Sometimes our greatest communication can be with God. "Pray always, that you may come off conqueror" (D&C 10:5).

Likewise, the mother who had been praying to have a better relationship with her struggling daughter experiences true joy when she shows up unannounced to a family party and trades hugs with her. Again, sometimes our greatest communication can be with God. "Pray always, and I will pour out my Spirit upon you" (D&C 19:38).

Our prayers and way of communicating will become inspired as we travel upwards in the way that we are living. Neal A. Maxwell said, "When we become sufficiently purified and cleansed from sin, we can ask what we will in the name of Jesus 'and it shall be done' (D&C 50:29). The Lord even promises us that when one reaches a certain spiritual condition, 'it shall be given you what you shall ask' (D&C 50:30)" (*All These Things Shall Give Thee Experience*, 95).

Therefore, in this new spiritual condition, we will not take things for granted anymore and will soon realize that our most important communication efforts should be with God. After all, it is He that will give us inspired "utterance" (Acts 2:4).

I remember when I first pulled all of the substances out of my body and how hard it was for me to communicate. I was having major trouble talking in front of people, and my social interactions seemed awkward. I remember praying often to God and asking Him to help me, but it wasn't until I started aligning my life with His that my communication and confidence improved. Thus my weaknesses became strengths.

That was a challenging time for me because I wanted it fixed quick. However, it took over a year's time for me to start feeling confident. During that time, I was presented with many opportunities to speak in front of people, and many times I failed and became horribly embarrassed. However, I kept going even when I could have bowed out. I figured that God was giving me these opportunities so that He could answer my prayers. Remember, we must meet Him halfway, and He will do the rest. He met me halfway by providing me with opportunities so that I could meet Him halfway.

The Lord can compensate for our communication weaknesses. Nephi wrote, "And the words which I have written in weakness will be made strong unto them; for it ... persuadeth them to believe in him, and to endure to the end" (2 Nephi 33:4, italics added).

Nephi had a preferred way of communicating, and understood the role of the Holy Ghost in helping him to be a better coach and missionary: "Neither am I [Nephi] mighty in writing, like unto speaking; for when a man speaketh by the power of the Holy Ghost the power of the Holy Ghost carrieth it unto the hearts of the children of men." (2 Nephi 33:1).

Be one who communicates often with the Head Coach in the School of Addiction, and be not afraid to share your time with Him!

The Psalmist exclaimed, "Exalt ye the Lord our God, and worship at his footstool; for he is holy" (Psalm 99:5).

PERSUASION INSTEAD OF MANIPULATION

Students in the School of Addiction seem to use people by manipulating to get what they want. T. S. Eliot said, "Half the harm that is done in this world is due to people who want to feel important. They don't mean to do harm—but the harm does not interest them. Or they do not see it, or they justify it because they are absorbed in the endless struggle to think well of themselves" (*The Cocktail Party*, Act 1, scene 1). It's so true that we are in a constant struggle to feel better about ourselves. However, when we are wrapped up in our addiction, a false self-esteem is created, which is then how we become liars and manipulators. We need to not be manipulators, but persuaders. Manipulation is often linked to lying, but persuasion is linked to coaching and God. If you are to become a good coach in the School of Addiction then you must become good at persuading, and only God can make us good at that.

Persuasion is defined as encouraging others to believe or do something by reasoning or pleading with them. In the Doctrine & Covenants, we are given some powerful advice on how to be good coaches:

> No power or influence can or ought to be maintained by virtue of the priesthood, only by persuasion, by long-suffering, by gentleness and meekness, and by love unfeigned;
>
> By kindness, and pure knowledge, which shall greatly enlarge the soul without hypocrisy, and without guile—
>
> Reproving betimes with sharpness, when moved upon by the Holy Ghost; and then showing forth afterwards an increase of love toward him whom thou hast reproved, lest he esteem thee to be his enemy. (D&C 121:41–43)

CREATE BETTER RELATIONSHIPS

Not only should we be good at persuading while teaching and coaching, but, more importantly, we must work on developing existing positive relationships into even better relationships by making that phone call, shooting over that text, or drafting up that letter or email. It's all about how large we can grow our circle of influence, which means we must seek to make good relationships even better relationships. The School of Addiction is all about being active in a community of like-minded individuals so that we can grow with one another. Go visit people, text people, serve people, and be friendly and happy. A smile can go such a long way. Get into the habit of smiling when walking into a room filled with people, and then watch what happens to your life.

Furthermore, we must commend people when they have done something good. Everybody wants to feel good about things, and when we tell someone they did a good job, it helps their light and self-esteem improve. Be happy for people even when they may have stolen the limelight from you. We all have our seasons in the School of Addiction, and when our season in the light finally passes and another student or coach takes our place, we should be happy for them as we move on to the next chapter. So many people need to be commended—and so do we. We should look for little opportunities to tell people they are doing a good job even though they may feel like the job they are currently doing could be done by just about anyone. Go ahead and step in to tell them good job so they can feel as if the job they are doing is special and could not be done just by anybody—only by them.

BE COACHABLE

We also must be coachable, which means allowing those who may have more faults than we to give us advice and counsel on occasion. There is nothing worse than when a friend throws helpful advice to his buddy, only to have it thrown back at him way below the belt. We all have stuff that we are not perfect at, and when someone offers us the hard advice, we cannot go on the defensive by looking for every fault of theirs and every reason to retaliate.

A homeless man, whom I helped to get sober when his family brought him back in for winter, ended up working for me around my gym facility. Oftentimes, he would offer me some hard advice concerning my business that I was not doing, and I remember going on the defensive. However, it was good advice, so I took it, and my program is now better because of it. Sometimes advice and beautiful counsel can come from those who have struggled the most.

CONCLUSION

From counseled to counselor we go, and from student to coach we can become. By communicating appropriately and offering and accepting counsel when needed, we will increase in knowledge and understanding concerning our own selves as well as the big picture of life. How wonderful life will become if we are solid in the way that we communicate with our friends and family, thus becoming "fishers of men" (Matthew 4:19).

CLASS 7
PRAYER

"And they did pray for that which they most desired; and they desired that the Holy Ghost should be given unto them."
3 Nephi 19:9

We have to be seeking help and guidance from the School of Addiction's Head Coach (Heavenly Father) daily if we are going to pass in the school. If we don't "pray always," then we will be tuned into the static stations instead of the clear sounding ones, even being "tempted by the devil, and . . . led away captive by him" (3 Nephi 18:15).

Why do some people have such a hard time with prayer? Is it because they can't see to whom they are praying? Is it because they can't see the reason behind it? Is it because it's not immediate?

ON HEAVENLY FATHER'S TIMETABLE

Neal A. Maxwell explains,

Petitioning in prayer has taught me, again and again, that the vault of heaven with all its blessings is to be opened only by a combination lock. One tumbler falls when there is faith; a second when there is personal righteousness; the third and final tumbler falls only when what is sought is, in God's judgment—not ours—right for us. Sometimes we pound on the vault door for something we want very much and wonder why the door does not open. We would be very spoiled children if that vault door opened any more easily than it does. I can tell, looking back, that God truly loves me by inventorying the petitions He has refused to grant me. Our rejected petitions tell us much about ourselves but also much about our flawless Father. ("Insights," *New Era*, April 1978)

In the School of Addiction, we want all the answers now, but unfortunately, that is not the way it goes, since the Lord has told us that "For my thoughts are not your thoughts, neither are your ways my ways" (Isaiah 55:8). Sometimes we might feel as if we are all alone, but if we can understand that the school's classes aren't always measured in the same way that we deal with time here in life, then our expectations can change. For example, the secular university classes are usually fifty minutes, but a class in the School of Addiction may take months, years, or even a lifetime. The sooner we can accept the truth that we are on God's calendar and not our own, then the sooner it is that He can lead us through the courses of the School of Addiction.

The Lord explained, "my words are sure and shall not fail. . . . But all things must come to pass in their time" (D&C 64:31–32).

It seems that sometimes God leaves us alone to do our own sorting out so that we might learn how to take the test on our own without Him by our side telling us the answers. "For he will give unto the faithful line upon line, precept upon precept; and I will try you and prove you herewith" (D&C 98:12).

There have been many times in the School of Addiction where I felt like the great tutor had left me alone only to later realize that I was being challenged with a learning experience that would greatly benefit me on down the road. I recall the time I couldn't stop making the call for opiates and had been praying to God the entire time for help but felt nothing. Then, out of the blue, I got a call from an old friend's mother who was like a second mother to me growing up, so she knew a thing or two about my struggle with addiction. This mother ended up referring me to a friend of hers who was a therapist that I have been working with ever since; a man sent from God who has helped me tremendously with not only my addiction but with my actual relationship with God as well. Maybe God was by my side the entire time; only I did not realize that I was on His timetable and not mine. "And ye must give thanks unto God in the Spirit for whatsoever blessing ye are blessed with" (D&C 46:32)..

CREATE PRAYER EXPERIENCES

I've had so many incredible prayer experiences that I can never deny. I recall a particular jog while listening to good music on a beautiful fall afternoon where I let gratitude and prayer engulf my heart and spirit until actual tears of joy rolled from my eyes. I remember the spring hike into the beautiful mountains where I had a few out loud conversations with God, expressing to Him my worries and concerns, but also sharing my gratitude for the wonderful life He has led me to live with my family. I think back on the intense weightlifting and conditioning workouts that hurt something awful, but afterward the high of gratitude for my physical health and ability rolls into my mind in which I am truly lifted. "It is a good thing to give thanks unto the Lord, and to sing praises unto thy name, O most High" (Psalm 92:1).

Prayer is a beautiful practice, and we shouldn't let anybody tell us otherwise. How beautiful it is to lead our children in prayer before bed and then for us to retire to our quiet spot in the house where we have our own prayer experience "to shew forth thy lovingkindness in the morning, and thy faithfulness every night" (Psalm 92:2). Or in the morning when just out of bed—where we go back to the same spot to plead for the protection of our family, for further guidance, and that "[our] wives and [our] children may be blessed" (3 Nephi 18:21). Or when the cravings become so intense that we have no other option but to get down on our knees and ask God to remove them so that we "may come off conqueror;

yea, that [we] may conquer Satan" (D&C 10:5). He will help us, if we "exercise [even] a particle of faith" (Alma 32:27) by having the courage to make a prayer experience happen during such a challenging time, and believing it will work, then "[He] will pour out [His] Spirit upon [us] in the day" (D&C 44:2).

PRAY FOR OTHERS

In this special school, we should hope and pray for the success of others. The coach should pray for his students, and likewise, the students should pray for one another and their coach. The tale of human nature is to hope for the failure of others. Misery loves company, right? Wrong! We will never succeed in this school if we are not all pulling for one another.

We are counseled to "love [our] enemies, bless them that curse [us], do good to them that hate [us], and pray for them which despitefully use [us], and persecute [us]" (Matthew 5:44).

The only way we will succeed in the School of Addiction is if others succeed since we are linked in special ways. Learn to pray for others even if you don't like them. At the end of the day, and when down on our knees in prayer, we must talk with God about any ill feelings that we may have toward others, and then we must make them right so that we can feel the peace of the Spirit. If we have too many contentions going on in our mind, then we are close to relapse. Pray for others, and you will be blessed with peace, confidence, and sobriety.

Having the belief that we are all children of a Father God that loves us is a great way to believe. In the book of Matthew, we learn of how a religious group tried to create contention for the Savior by asking Him a tough question. "Master," they asked Him, "which is the great commandment in the law?" Jesus answered,

> Thou shalt love the Lord thy God with all thy heart, and with all thy soul, and with all thy mind.
>
> This is the first and great commandment.
>
> And the second is like unto it, Thou shalt love thy neighbour as thyself.

On these two commandments hang all the law and the prophets. (Matthew 22:36–40)

Can we really love our neighbor if we do not first love God? God is love, and if we forget about Him, then how can we love anything other than ourselves?

When relapse happens for me, I am mostly upset because of how I disappointed God. And the times when I've been fully lost in relapse, all love and charity seem to leave my heart. This makes it impossible for me to love my neighbor because I'm too much in love with myself.

Therefore, we have to be the one who prays for opportunities to serve in someone else's life. When an opportunity to serve arises, we should jump on it quickly and with no hesitation, all while giving thanks to God for providing us with an opportunity to feel better about ourselves. "And they did pray for that which they most desired; and they desired that the Holy Ghost should be given unto them" (3 Nephi 19:9).

We need to feel good about ourselves quite often, and if we don't feel good about who we are and what we are doing, then we might find ourselves looking for that false pleasure that got us into trouble in the first place. So in our petitioning, let's ask for opportunities to serve and create in another person's life so that the creation of self-worth happens in our own lives. It is the process of losing ourselves in the service of others where we find ourselves. "For whosoever will save his life shall lose it: and whosoever will lose his life for my sake shall find it" (Matthew 16:25).

THE GOSPEL VALUES AND AN OLD LABRADOR

Have you ever noticed that our values soon become our addiction's values instead of our Heavenly Father's? Growing up, we were taught right from wrong, and stealing, lying, and manipulating were bad. However, when wrapped up in our addictions, stealing, lying, and manipulating soon become an option, "for after this manner doth the devil work" (Moroni 7:17).

We need prayer to help us find our core values. We need to travel into a way of life that is full of prayer and meditation experiences so that we can find ourselves being grateful for the sunsets again. When lost in our addictions, we forget how to be grateful for even the smallest of life's experiences, "for [Satan] persuadeth no man to do good, no, not one; neither do his angels" (Moroni 7:17). Everything is an experience when we are sober since we are now on the high roads of life as opposed to being on the back shallow roads of our addiction.

I had an awesome experience not long ago with my grandpa and my dad's old Labrador that taught me a great lesson about not taking for granted any of life's experiences, and that even in unusual circumstances, there are always lessons to be learned.

My father had an old Lab named Jackson who was fifteen years old and at the age where he was suffering and couldn't walk. My father was then out of town and gave the job of watching over Jackson to my grandpa. My dad had hoped his friend would have a few more months of life, but that didn't end up being the case.

On the first night of his watch, my grandpa went over to my dad's house to feed Jackson and found him lying under a tree, unable to walk or even raise his head. He then called my dad and gave him the news; my father gave the go-ahead for Grandpa and me to put Jackson to sleep.

The following morning, my grandfather and I pulled up to the vet clinic. As they prepared for Jackson, my grandpa and I had a conversation that I will never forget. He seemed upset, and his eyes were swelling with sadness and tears. I soon realized that it was not so much the idea of Jackson being put to sleep that was causing him to be emotional as much as it was his link to Jackson's old age. My grandpa, being eighty-three years old, went on to tell me that he felt he had about seven years of life remaining and then explained how seven years may seem like a long time to a young man like me, but at his age it is a blink of an eye, and would come in no time. He told me that he was not scared to experience death because he felt he had done the best he could in this life, and he was prepared to meet God in the next life.

As Jackson's euthanasia process proceeded, and as we watched our beloved friend take his last breath, my grandpa and I hugged in a warm embrace with both of us crying. We were saddened by the loss of Jackson, but there was something deeper that was influencing our emotions. Maybe it was the glimpse back through the veil that Jackson helped us see. His death showed both of us the eternal family picture by giving us a further hope and understanding that families can be together forever; not just our human family, but our pet family, as well. Maybe this experience with Jackson helped us to appreciate our family more fully and to not take advantage of time but to use it wisely and honorably by being family- and service-oriented instead of worldly and selfish.

I learned a great lesson that day. And though Jackson will be missed, I'm thankful for what he and my grandfather taught me. Sometimes we learn in the most unique ways, and if we are too wrapped up in the world, then we will miss what God is trying to tell us.

CONCLUSION

If we are not in tune with the spiritual way of life, then it will be hard for us to notice important life experiences. We must take the time to work on prayer in the morning, throughout the day, and at night so that we can be led to finding gratitude for all things. We should pray for insight on how to balance our lives and families so that we can create reverence and peace within our home environments. We should pray to remove any contention and ill feelings we may have toward others. We should pray for the ability to endure and to recognize when God is trying to teach us something—though I need to remind you, on His timetable.

And lastly, we must walk this life supporting a lifestyle that is healthy—physically, mentally, morally, and spiritually— so that our prayers will not be drowned out by all the noise from the world.

Get into prayer so that you can find gratitude. Get into prayer so that you can find out who you truly are and what you are capable of in the School of Addiction.

QUIET STRENGTH

"And the remission of sins bringeth meekness, and lowliness of heart; and because of meekness and lowliness of heart cometh the visitation of the Holy Ghost, which Comforter filleth with hope and perfect love."

Moroni 8:26

At the Huntsman Cancer Institute, I worked for a doctor for whom I have a great amount of respect. He was the chief of surgery and head of the pancreas cancer research program, and was a man who was highly respected and recognized all over the world for his incredible work. I remember watching this man transition from performing a five-hour surgery to sitting through meeting after meeting. I was blown away by how he worked. He never seemed to be in a rush, nor did he ever act like he was too busy or tired, even though he was probably the busiest, most tired man in the building. His walk was slow and casual, and during meetings, he would allow others to talk first while he patiently listened, but he would offer counsel and even wise reproof when needed. He was friendly, compassionate, patient, and humble, and seemed to be full of love and gratitude. This man was meek but firm.

Another man whom I study and admire is a therapist that I was led to early on that helped me find the gospel of Jesus Christ and myself. This is the man that I still work with today. This man has held various high callings in the Church of Jesus Christ of Latter-day Saints, and he is someone that I hope to one day emulate. He is friendly, compassionate, patient, humble, and full of love and gratitude. This man is also meek but very firm.

I, too, want to one day carry the character of being meek and firm, and so should you. If we are meek, then we are coachable, teachable, and likable. If we are meek, we don't talk behind other people's backs, nor do we complain, since we are carrying the "meek and quiet spirit" (1 Peter 3:4). If we are meek, we can deal with the uncomfortable times of the moment because our character will be strong and reserved, as opposed to being loud and loose. If we are meek, we are tough and confident and cannot be acted upon.

These few men—and there are others—have helped shape a vision of the type of man I hope to one day become. I want to be the man who can carry a spiritual presence that commands respect. I want to be caring and loving but also have the ability to get after someone when they are out of line. I've had many coaches over the years who would get after me when I made a mistake in a game, only to lift me up by telling me how good of a job I had done in the other areas of the game.

Jesus talked of Himself as being "meek and lowly in heart" (Matthew 11:29). Paul praised the "meekness and gentleness of Christ" (2 Corinthians 10:1). In the New Testament, the definition of meek is "gentle and humble."

Elder Neal A. Maxwell explained,

Meekness is not an attribute which is essential only in itself. . . . It is also vital because one cannot develop those other crucial virtues—faith, hope, and charity—without meekness.

In the ecology of the eternal attributes, these cardinal characteristics are inextricably bound up together. Among them, meekness is often the initiator, facilitator, and consolidator.

In fact, if one needs any further persuasion as to how vital this virtue is, Moroni warned, "none is acceptable before God, save the meek and lowly in heart." (Moroni 7:43–44.) If we could but believe, really believe, in the reality of that bold but accurate declaration, you and I would find ourselves focusing on the crucial rather than the marginal tasks in life! We would then cease pursuing lifestyles which, inevitably and irrevocably, are going out of style! ("Meekness—A Dimension of True Discipleship," *Ensign*, March 1983)

MEEK PAHORAN AND MORONI

In the Book of Mormon, we read of an exchange that takes place between Moroni, the chief captain of the armies, and Pahoran, who was chief judge and governor of the land during a time of war (Alma 60–61). Moroni seemed to be upset and was complaining to Pahoran about a scenario that he had created in his mind about the reason for Pahoran not sending help and provisions. Pahoran's reply becomes a priceless learning experience for us on how to remain meek.

Moroni wrote to Pahoran, desiring "to know the cause of this exceedingly great neglect; yea, we desire to know the cause of your thoughtless state" (Alma 60:6). Moroni had built out in his mind the scenario of Pahoran and his team sitting "upon [their] thrones in a state of thoughtless stupor" (Alma 60:7), and not doing much at all to help his army, but instead sitting back in the comfort of government office to watch "thousands [fall] by the sword" (Alma 60:8). Moroni then took a hard jab at Pahoran and his team by saying, "We know not but what ye are also traitors to your country" (Alma 60:18). And that he (Pahoran) had better "administer . . . relief," or Moroni would "come unto [him] . . . and smite [him] with the sword" (Alma 60:30).

Pahoran, who was the chief judge and governor of the land, then makes this meek reply to his chief captain by saying, "Behold, I say unto you, Moroni, that I do not joy in your great afflictions, yea, it grieves my soul" (Alma 61:2). In the epistle, Pahoran tells Moroni of the insurrection and rebellion against the government and that this was the reason for him not being able to send support. "And behold, they have driven me out before them, and I [Pahoran] have fled to the land of Gideon, with as many men as it were possible that I could get." (Alma 61:5). And then Pahoran makes the meekest gesture of all: "And now, in your epistle you have censured me, but it mattereth not; I am not angry, but do rejoice in the greatness of your heart. I, Pahoran, do not seek for power, save only to retain my judgment-seat that I may preserve the rights and the liberty of my people. My soul standeth fast in that liberty in the which God hath made us free." (Alma 61:9).

We can all learn a great lesson from this story on the importance of remaining meek, since resentments are what kill the Spirit. And if we have not the Holy Spirit with us at all times, and are walking around with contention swelling in our minds for people, then it is only a matter of time before we say or do something that we will regret. Most of the problems for the addict stem from building out false scenarios in our minds that lead to massive thinking errors and finally resentments. If we want to change our behavior, then we must change the way that we think. That means trying to see the best in people instead of their worst.

STOP FEELING SORRY

Everyone has challenging life events that they are dealing with. Whatever is going on inside any given person's mind that is causing them stress is a big deal to them, regardless of how severe it may appear to the next guy. One person may be battling with pill addiction, while another person might be dealing with mild depression. Both people, in their own minds, are struggling with severe problems, regardless of what they both think of each other, which means there is no room for judgment. We can't think that our problems are worse off than everybody else's or that we are more special and important because of what we are dealing with when compared to what they are dealing with. The trick is that we must seek to have empathy for others so that we can stop feeling sorry for our own selves. We need to remain "meek and lowly."

There are a few things you can control in this life, one major one being how you choose to view the world, among much more. If you say you are unhealthy and unhappy, well then, what are you going to do about it? It's unacceptable to just complain and try to get everyone to feel sorry for you. Instead, go to work on the things you can control, like your attitude, nutrition, getting more exercise, reading and studying the scriptures, and watching less TV. Good things happen to those who replace poor habits with healthy habits. This is a true principle that will work for everybody, so stop feeling sorry for yourself and go to work on being healthier. And just remember, at the end of the day, nobody can change for you except it be you.

What people will care about is your new found positive tone. They like it that your focus has switched from off of yourself and onto others. Now the question remains of how consistent can you be at doing this? It's easy to stay positive and charitable when things are peachy, but it's not so easy when the stresses of life come after you. And they will come, because life seems to be filled with rainier days than sunny ones, so get used to it.

Jenkin Lloyd Jones said,

Anyone who imagines that bliss is normal is going to waste a lot of time running around shouting that he has been robbed. Most putts don't drop. Most beef is tough. Most children grow up to be just people. Most successful marriages require a high degree of mutual toleration. Most jobs are more often dull than otherwise. . . . Life is like an old-time rail journey—delays, sidetracks, smoke, dust, cinders and jolts, interspersed only occasionally by beautiful vistas and thrilling bursts of speed. The trick is to thank the Lord for letting you have the ride. ("Big Rock Candy Mountains," Deseret News, 12 June, 1973)

SPIRITUAL GROWTH

It seems as if there are seasons to life. "To every thing there is a season, and a time to every purpose under the heaven" (Ecclesiastes 3:1). Our physical season may grow from our early twenties into our forties, but then our physical season starts to die down and our spiritual season continues to grow—even more so as our body gets old. That is the beauty about developing our spiritual character: we can keep on developing it no matter what happens to our physical body. We can only lifts weights and play sports competitively for so long before our body tells us that swimming, hiking, walking, and biking are our new sports.

Elder Quentin L. Cook explained,

Physical, mental, and spiritual development have much in common. Physical development is fairly easy to see. We begin with baby steps and progress day by day, year by year, growing and developing to attain our ultimate physical stature. Development is different for each person. . . .

Most people recognize that to obtain peak physical and mental performance, such preparation and practice are essential.

Unfortunately, in an increasingly secular world, less emphasis is placed on the amount of spiritual growth necessary to become more Christlike and establish the foundations that lead to enduring faith. We tend to emphasize moments of sublime spiritual understanding. These are precious instances when we know the Holy Ghost has witnessed special spiritual insights to our hearts and minds. We rejoice in these events; they should not be diminished in any way. But for enduring faith and to have the constant companionship of the Spirit, there is no substitute for the individual religious observance that is comparable to physical and mental development. We should build on these experiences, which sometimes resemble initial baby steps. We do this by consecrated commitment to sacred sacrament meetings, scripture study, prayer, and serving as called. ("Foundations of Faith," *Ensign*, May 2017)

It seems, then, that our spiritual growth is endless, and if we work hard on developing a meek character, then we, too, will "walk as children of light" (Ephesians 5:8), even being able to command respect in our later years because of how far our spiritual condition will have come. "For ye were sometimes darkness, but now are ye light in the Lord" (Ephesians 5:8). However, if we just keep moving along, being drug addicts who aren't seeking to change nor obtain the virtues of knowledge, meekness, patience, temperance, and much more, then we will grow old and be without. This is all hard advice, I know—but it's the truth, and you need to hear it!

FEARLESS AND FAITH

Our fears can be managed if we can bring ourselves to being meek and poised. Again, being meek means we are in control of how we act, what we think about, and how we speak. Profanity isn't in line with being meek, nor is losing our composure in traffic. Meekness, then, offsets our fears by helping us to feel in control of ourselves since we will feel spiritual and reverent throughout our days, even delighting ourselves "in the abundance of peace" (Psalm 37:11). Basically, meekness gives us confidence by how it is linked to our faith. We now believe in inspiration and revelation and are able to be taught from on high. We are teachable! "For the Lord taketh pleasure in his people: he will beautify the meek with salvation" (Psalm 149:4).

Step 3 of the 12 steps reminds us to turn our lives over to the care of God the Eternal Father and His Son, Jesus Christ, and to fear not the clear life. But why do so many of us fear the clear life? Is it because the clear life is so simple and a bit monotonous? Is it that we look forward to the night and don't see much excitement, so we crave the escape, thinking that it will make it more exciting? But if we then choose to escape, it won't last long, and shame, fear, and guilt are sure to follow. Whereas if we remained clear and got through what we thought was not exciting, we would have realized that it was far more exciting, and that our mood is now full of peace and charity because of our good decision to remain clear. Jesus said, "Peace I give unto you. . . . Let not your heart be troubled, neither let it be afraid" (John 14:27).

It just requires us to have faith that we can make it through the weekend. And yes, our mood will falter, and cravings will most definitely enter at some point. But if we will hold tight and lean upon God by taking His yoke upon us, then our way will be made light, "and ye shall find rest unto your souls" (Matthew 11:29). This will give us strength for next week's battle so that we can, once again, "come off conqueror" (D&C 10:5).

Each weekend will get a little bit easier, though our patience and temperance will be tested so that we might obtain these attributes into our character as well. We cannot expect to fill the holes in our character if we are not challenged by those things that make us weak. The Lord said, "I give unto men weakness that they may be humble." And the only way to grow is to overcome what we are afraid of; and due to us being on pause for all of those years, we, unfortunately, have a lot of work to do on our character. But if we will have "faith in [God], then will [He] make weak things become strong" (Ether 12:27)..

WALK EACH DAY IN REVERENCE

I like the idea of trying to walk each day in reverence. This means that we don't allow a busy day to cause us to act busy and stressed. This means that we are able to take hour-long naps at lunch since we worked hard all morning. I hate it when people try to act busy in an effort to impress others. How can we be meek and successful in the School of Addiction if we are always acting stressed and busy? We should remain calm and lean upon God for support "and see that all these things are done in wisdom and order; for it is not requisite that a man should run faster than he has strength (Mosiah 4:27). Low-key and poised is the type of character we are looking for, along with being a hard and smart worker who can communicate effectively and boldly.

I have found that if I work on having this meek and lowly character, I have fewer cravings. And when I do have cravings, I am better able to handle them.

Remember, we don't need to always be doing something crazy and fun. It's okay to spend an afternoon reading, studying, and hanging out with family. We cannot let our moods get the best of us. If we are meek, then they won't. We have to learn to enjoy the simple, and that means reading, writing, and going for an afternoon jog. Over time, you will come to love doing this. That is why we must develop a meek and humble character so that we can come to appreciate the simple things in life. Things like the wind blowing in the trees on a summer night or the Sunday morning walks with the family in the spring. Meekness teaches us to appreciate all moments.

MENTAL TOUGHNESS

It is true that we are not that tough on our own: we are only as tough as the amount of spiritual in our system. The spiritual amount is linked to how meek and obedient we are. If we are living poorly and loudly, then our spiritual gas tank will be empty and running on fumes, since "a fool uttereth all his mind: but a wise man keepeth it in till afterwards" (Proverbs 29:11).

Therefore, if we are living meekly and lowly, then our spiritual gas tank will be full of the premium blend and will assist us in enduring the tough terrain of life, even making us tough in our mind.

We secretly applaud those individuals who are dealing with life situations that are far tougher than ours. For example, the father of two children who were born handicapped and who looks upon his situation as being one that is blessed by how he is able to participate in raising special children, believing that he will be able to learn from those two children. The experience is making him a better father, husband, and human being. Well, this man carries a special type of strength. This man is meek.

Then there is the mother who has lost her four-year-old son in a car accident and is dealing with heartache and sadness. She moves forward valiantly and with faith in her heart that she will see her son again in the hereafter. She believes that all is well with him, so all should be well with her. This woman carries a special type of strength. This woman is meek.

On our own, we are not that tough, but when we are locked into experiencing God's rhythm working within our lives, we can again "come off conqueror" (D&C 10:5). A new toughness will arise within us, making those tough life situations seem not so tough. Now when we feel the stress of being burdened financially, we can lean upon God with faith and hope that He is helping us to improve our character and way of life so that we can improve our financial situation. His strength makes it so that the light within our soul will be bright, and now every potential employer that we are interviewing with will clearly see where we might be of use to them.

The low-level job becomes an endurance test, especially for the employee who feels that the job is too low for him when previously he had a higher job. Now he is forced to work this lower job, which causes a poor attitude and feelings of embarrassment. When people ask him about his life and job, he downplays the job and makes excuses as to why he has it. This employee is not meek.

What this employee should do is be thankful for the opportunity to have a job and realize that even though he may have been overqualified for the job in the past, he is not overqualified now. No matter what his reasons are for having this new job, he is just the same as everyone else, and should be thankful for the opportunity. He must be meek.

This takes mental toughness. Nobody wants to admit they are in a lower position than they once were. However, we can travel upwards in our job if we show up on-time, strive to learn as much as we can, and look to create new and healthy relationships each day. We need to be dependable! And when we say we are going to do something, then we need to do it. There is no room for excuses anymore as those are consistent practices of one who is using drugs and alcohol. We are not using drugs and alcohol anymore, so we must work on being someone who can be trusted. We must be meek and reliable.

QUIT SELF PITY AND IMPATIENCE

Just because we feel discomfort each day does not mean our life is bad. Don't let some bad experiences in the day cause you to complain about your life in a tone of self-pity. For example, we can be part of those at work who are complaining with the other employees about how bad their boss and job sucks. Or we can choose to stay out of such circles and be happy with our opportunity to be working. We can choose to be meek. We can choose to be thankful for one more day of sobriety and the job that we have.

Remember, self-pity will hold us back in our progression as a human being. It's quite hard to grow our character upwards if we are always caught in the downward spiral of self-pity and shame. When walking into a room, we should throw a smile on our face and strive to share in beautiful conversations with others that are positive and uplifting. There is nothing worse than the person who can't be spoken to without them stating all of their self-pity problems. Such people become energy vampires, and before long their circle of influence will dissolve. Nobody wants to be brought down with another sad story, so don't be the one who is always sharing their sad stories. No progress can be made on such a path, and I know this to be true because I have been on that path.

It's a pathetic practice when we find ourselves being impatient with the faults and weaknesses of others. We become unlikable in this instance and are oftentimes looked upon as being worse than an immature child. Such a flaw will lead those around us to become impatient as well since our poor example will have caused frustration in their lives, and is now causing them to lose their patience. Likewise, if our patience is constantly being lost in front of our children and family members, then we will have helped create an impatient family by allowing our impatience to spread to them. We have got to remember that all people are imperfect, including us. Again, hard advice, but you need to hear it.

CONCLUSION

Let's be meek and patient people. Let's carry the type of quiet strength that doesn't need to be heard but can be felt. Let's give people the benefit of the doubt, and when we walk into a room full of people, let's be smiling and approachable. Let's be forgiving of others even when it might be hard to forgive. And more importantly, let's be patient with ourselves as we fumble along in the classes of the great School of Addiction.

CLASS 9
FORGIVING

"Behold, he who has repented of his sins, the same is forgiven, and I, the Lord, remember them no more."

D&C 58:42

How beautiful it is when someone who lost trust in you finds trust again. Likewise, how beautiful it is when you now trust and like your own self. This forgiving class in the School of Addiction will tell us that we must seek forgiveness from others, ourselves, and, of course, God. But, more importantly, we must also be forgiving of those who may have done us wrong.

Let's be honest: we have manipulated and done may shady things during our addiction career, so there is no need to further elaborate on what all we may have done or whom we have hurt. We just need to figure out what we need to do to make things right. "But as oft as they repented and sought forgiveness, with real intent, they were forgiven" (Moroni 6:8).

In King Benjamin's magnificent sermon, "which had been delivered unto him by the angel of the Lord" and brought the people to a recollection of their own sins, his words struck them so deeply that "they had fallen to the earth, for the fear of the Lord had come upon them" (Mosiah 4:1). And because of the Spirit carrying his words to them, they were taught how important it was for them to repent and live their religion (Mosiah 4:2).

When we get lost in the world of drug and alcohol addiction for a long period of time, we become "past feeling," and don't realize the type of people that we have become. And then when we finally do clear up, it becomes evident to us of how lost we truly were, since we now view ourselves in our "own carnal state" (Mosiah 4:2).

The repentance process is full of humility, prayer, and tears, as was the case for King Benjamin's people: "And they all cried aloud with one voice, saying: O have mercy, and apply the atoning blood of Christ that we may receive forgiveness of our sins, and our hearts may be purified; for we believe in Jesus Christ, the Son of God, who created heaven and earth, and all things; who shall come down among the children of men" (Mosiah 4:2)

Just as in step three of the 12 steps, King Benjamin's people decided to turn their wills and lives over to the care of God the Eternal Father and His Son, Jesus Christ. The people now accepted the Atonement of Jesus Christ and "filled with joy, having received a remission of their sins, and having peace of conscience, because of the exceeding faith which they had in Jesus Christ" (Mosiah 4:3).

BROKEN HEART AND CONFESSION

In order to obtain this forgiveness for our sins, we must first have a "broken heart and a contrite spirit" (3 Nephi 9:20) for the poor way of life that we have been leading. And then we must recommit ourselves to living a better life by repenting in prayer to the Lord and confessing to our bishop, thus giving us an accountability partner here on Earth. "By this ye may know if a man repenteth of his sins—behold, he will confess them and forsake them" (D&C 58:43).

It takes courage to walk into a bishop's office to tell him who you are and what you have done—I know it did for me. Maybe you have broken some of those covenants you made in the past to the Church, which led you to getting excommunicated or disfellowshipped. How embarrassing, right? Wrong! How courageous of you to come in and make it right!

You had the courage to walk into the bishop's office, being meek and ready to make the long walk back to the "strait and narrow course" (Helaman 3:29). Again, this takes courage, and many will just play along on the sidelines, hiding their talents for fear of embarrassment instead of getting back into the game. Or worse yet, they will throw rocks at the gospel, even trying to convince themselves that the gospel of Jesus Christ isn't right for them anymore. Remember, it's far easier to be a coach in the stands than it is to be an actual player in the game.

Even inside the traditional 12-step program, there is a confession step where we "admit to God, to ourselves, and to another human being the exact nature of our wrongs." This step allows us to confess our sins to another person so that growth can be captured and an accountability partner can be gained.

JUSTICE AND MERCY

God, therefore, has a set of rules that He asks us to follow, and when we break those rules, there are consequences. "Whosoever, therefore, shall break one of these least commandments, and shall teach men so to do, he shall in no wise be saved in the kingdom of heaven" (JST, Matthew 5:21). However, God has made mercy available through the atoning sacrifice of His Son, Jesus Christ, who paved the way for a repentance process when He voluntarily competed on our behalf in the School of Addiction by taking upon Him "the sins of the world, to bring about the plan of mercy, to appease the demands of justice, that God might be a perfect, just God, and a merciful God also" (Alma 42:15).

For example, if we get a DUI and cause harm to another person by getting in a wreck, then we must pay our debt to society before we can receive mercy, freedom, and forgiveness. Likewise, we must pay our debt to God before He can offer His mercy to us.

Let's say we turned our will and life over to the care of God the Eternal Father and His Son, Jesus Christ, and repented of our many sins. But as time moved forward, we ended up being complacent and once again returned to being dishonest drug addicts who took advantage of people for the remainder of our lives, even dying in our sins. This means that we did not finish the game. And regardless of how well we might have played in the beginning or middle of the game matters not, since the only thing that matters is how we finished.

Furthermore, in a football game, one might have the game of his life all the way up until the fourth quarter when he fumbles in the opponents' end zone to lose the game. Yes, he played well throughout the entire game, but lost focus at the end and fell short when it counted.

Now, I realize there are those who have competed with themselves to the best of their ability and still end up getting tripped up by the addiction disease. And these aren't the people I'm speaking of; struggling with relapse and constantly fighting to get back on track with the help of God isn't the same thing as giving up altogether. Point being is that we must stay competing with ourselves for the entirety of our lives, and we cannot think that the full abundant life will be handed to us without work. "And he said unto me, My grace is sufficient for thee: for my strength is made perfect in weakness. Most gladly therefore will I rather glory in my infirmities, that the power of Christ may rest upon me" (2 Corinthians 12:9).

You see, all of our blessings are dependent on our obedience to the commandments since "there is a law, irrevocably decreed in heaven before the foundations of this world, upon which all blessings are predicated (D&C 130:20). And when we lose focus and drop the ball, we must repent.

Elder D. Todd Christofferson said,

God will always love us, but He cannot save us in our sins. Remember the words of Amulek to Zeezrom that the Savior would not save His people in their sins but from their sins, the reason being that with sin we are unclean and 'no unclean thing can inherit the kingdom of heaven' or dwell in God's presence. 'And [Christ] hath power given unto him from the Father to redeem [His people] from their sins because of repentance; therefore he hath sent his angels to declare the tidings of the conditions of repentance, which bringeth unto the power of the Redeemer, unto the salvation of their souls.'

From the Book of Mormon we learn that the intent of Christ's suffering—the ultimate manifestation of His love—was 'to bring about the bowels of mercy, which overpowereth justice, and bringeth about means unto men that they may have faith unto repentance.

"And thus mercy can satisfy the demands of justice, and encircles them in the arms of safety, while he that exercises no faith unto repentance is exposed to the whole law of the demands of justice; therefore only unto him that has faith unto repentance is brought about the great and eternal plan of redemption."

Repentance, then, is His gift to us, purchased at a very dear price. ("Abide In My Love," Ensign, November 2016)

ACCOUNTABILITY PARTNER

God holds us accountable but has also made a way to forgive us "only on conditions of repentance" (Alma 42:13). God has to hold us accountable for how we are living, or why would we care to change? If He just forgave us all the time without requiring a sacrifice from us, then why would we ever feel that we needed Him? If God were just a pushover, then it would be hard to respect Him. No one respects the person who lets everybody walk all over them—so why would it be any different with God and His Son, Jesus Christ?

As addicts, we need this high level of accountability that the gospel of Jesus Christ offers. We need to feel sadness when we offend the Spirit because that shows our love for Him.

Remember, we have to be carrying a severely "broken heart and contrite spirit" for the way that we have been acting, and only then can the repentance process move forward. It doesn't happen in a day, nor even a year. It takes diligence to living the commandments before we "may be found spotless, pure, fair, and white, having been cleansed by the blood of the Lamb" (Mormon 9:6).

"Behold, he who has repented of his sins, the same is forgiven, and I, the Lord, remember them no more" (D&C 58:42).

"But learn that he who doeth the works of righteousness shall receive his reward, even peace in this world, and eternal life in the world to come" (D&C 59:23).

WORKING HARD ON OUR RECOVERY

We need to show people, and ourselves, that we are hard workers in the School of Addiction. If we want the forgiveness and trust of our family members and friends, then we must show them that we are working hard each day on our recovery. This means that we are going to our addiction recovery meetings (AA, NA, ARP), exercising daily, trying to eat healthy, reading out of the best books, and are remaining humble, meek, and lowly, among much more. This means that not one second of our day is wasted on things that don't matter, things like sleeping in, watching too much TV, playing video games, and just being an all-around lazy human being.

When I was first trying to change my life, I was working as a full-time administrator at a prestigious cancer center. I was scared, because for so long I was doing my job high. Now that I wasn't, things were different because I didn't have a clue who I was. During this time, I started being a reader about Christ and would leave on my breaks to read, study, and even write. At night, I was lifting weights, reading, and trying to remain present around my family. I found prayer during this time along with the Church's addiction recovery meetings, therapy, and nutrition. I held true to this routine, and the people around me, like my wife, kids, parents, and friends, all seemed to appreciate what I was doing, and this felt good to me. Over time, I started liking who I was becoming, which caused me to become further motivated.

My story shows how you have the opportunity to be inspiring in the lives of others if you start doing well in the School of Addiction. Let's be honest: no one expects much out of the struggling student because, more times than not, they stay a struggling student. However, if the struggling student starts working hard and improves his grades from Fs to As—well, now everybody is impressed and happy. Most people will forgive us if we change our lives. If we change our lives in a big way, we will end up inspiring those around us, and they, too, will have a desire to improve. A lot of people in the world don't think people can change, and the one who has been at the bottom for a long time does have a long way to go; so when she goes from the bottom to the top, it becomes a beautiful site to see.

Remember, it's easy to talk about changing, but it's another thing to actually do it. I've seen many people come through my doors talking the talk, but never end up having the courage to walk the walk. In fact, they don't talk at all—they just start walking and doing. Keep a steady pace and pressure on your studies in the School of Addiction, and before long you will be moving on to the next class. Be a hard worker!

CHRIST FORGAVE EVERYONE

People will forgive you and so will God! In the New Testament, Luke records a story about how Jesus was invited to Simon's home for dinner (see Luke 7:36–50). There then came a sinful woman who "knew that Jesus sat at meat in [Simon's] house, [and] brought an alabaster box of ointment" (Luke 7:37). As Jesus rested, this woman then "stood at his feet behind him weeping, and began to wash his feet with tears, and did wipe them with the hairs of her head, and kissed his feet, and anointed them with the ointment" (Luke 7:38). Simon then became mad, even finding fault with Jesus for allowing a sinner to serve Him.

Jesus then went on to teach Simon a beautiful lesson on forgiveness when he told the story of a creditor who had two debtors. The one debtor owed 500 pence, and the other 50. Neither of them could pay their debts, so the creditor forgave them both. "Tell me therefore," the Savior asked, "which of [the debtors] will love [the creditor] most?" (Luke 7:42). Simon answered that the debtor who owed the most would love the most.

Jesus was impressed with the woman's behavior and saw that her heart was good. The point of the story was for Simon to see himself as being the debtor who owed less and the woman as the debtor who owed more. Jesus then said, "Wherefore I say unto thee, Her sins, which are many, are forgiven; for she loved much: but to whom little is forgiven, the same loveth little" (Luke 7:47).

Jesus then said, "thy sins are forgiven. . . . Thy faith hath saved thee; go in peace" (Luke 7:48, 50; see also Cecil O. Samuelson Jr., "Words of Jesus: Forgiveness," *Ensign*, February 2003).

Can you imagine the peace that this woman must have felt after being forgiven of her many sins? We too can go in peace if we will come unto the Savior and love much (Luke 7:47). We can learn a great deal from this woman by how she decided to turn her will and life over to the care of God the Eternal Father and His Son, Jesus Christ. He forgave her! And likewise, He will forgive us!

In the New Testament, Christ forgave everyone, including those who crucified Him, when He said, "Father, forgive them; for they know not what they do" (Luke 23:34). When I am doing bad and struggling with my addiction, I often feel that God is disappointed in me because He knows I can do better, but never do I feel like He will not forgive me. Instead, I feel like He's saying, "Come on, man, you'll be alright. Let's get back on track. Keep fighting and look at this relapse as being a learning experience that will make you stronger. You can do it! Be a hard worker! Let's go! Keep reading, praying, exercising, and studying. You'll be okay. I love you." Is it not the same with our own parents? My dad has been disappointed with me, but he has always had my back no matter what it is that I do, and the same goes for me being a forgiving and helpful father to my own children.

CHRIST IS OUR COACH

I see Christ as being our coach in the School of Addiction who is forgiving, loving, and caring, but not always tolerant, just as He was not tolerant to those "found in the temple those that sold oxen and sheep and doves" (John 2:14) for money and to get gain. He ended up driving these people out of the temple "and poured out the changers' money, and overthrew the tables" (John 2:15). Jesus said firmly, "Take these things hence; make not my Father's house an house of merchandise" (John 2:16).

Christ asks us to compete for Him in the School of Addiction, which means we cannot just hear and except the plays without trying to run them. Instead, we must be performers by seeking to be "perfect, even as [our] father which is in heaven is perfect" (Matthew 5:48). We must carry out His plays or we will end up getting benched! If we do get benched, however, that does not mean that Christ does not love or care for us; but it does mean that we have to "prove [ourselves] herewith" (D&C 98:12) before He will put us back into the game, which He always will because that is His promise to us. "And whomsoever ye receive shall believe in my name; and him will I freely forgive" (Mosiah 26:22).

Sometimes it's a good thing to get benched because it may lead us to having a recollection of how good it was to be in the game with Christ. Now that we are not in the game, we can tell the difference between the peace of the Spirit and the chaos of the world, which causes us to compete even harder with ourselves in an effort to get back in the game. And now that we are back in the game, we have an even stronger desire to stay competing because we now know the difference.

FORGIVING OURSELVES

Forgiving ourselves can be quite the challenge, but remember that shame will only keep us lost in the school's halls. It is the same concept when it comes to forgiving ourselves: if we walk the walk and work hard, then we will start feeling good about ourselves, and there will be no room for shame and regret. Yes, being contrite and saddened may last awhile, but such feelings as these are healthy since they will lead us to be motivated and determined. Over time, you will be okay with yourself. However, you will not even come close to feeling okay if you cannot move forward. You must leave the past behind! Again, you must leave the past behind! Dwelling on the past will keep us in our past addictive ways. And letting the past go will free us to experience a bright future. Just get motivated to improve upon your character by getting lost in hard work and service to others, and there will be no room for shame.

Neal A. Maxwell counseled, "Motivation can arise out of humiliation, just as determination can grow out of deprivation" (*Notwithstanding My Weakness*, [Salt Lake City: Deseret Book, 1981]).

Like Alma, we can be completely forgiven and be "harrowed up by the memory of [our] sins no more" (Alma 36:19). We will still have the memories of our past mistakes, but they will be softened and made easier to bear once we are secured to Christ's foundation, "which is a sure foundation, a foundation whereon if men build they cannot fall" (Helaman 5:12). After all, nobody becomes inspiring in the lives of others if their walk in life was smooth and easy.

FORGIVING OF OTHERS

We need to be forgiving of others if we are expecting others to forgive us. If you are holding contention and madness for another person, then this is not a good mind frame to be in since contention will lower our spiritual condition. Remember, our sobriety is dependent on our spiritual condition, and if we have ill feelings toward another person, then it will be hard to experience the peace of sobriety. When our mind is racing with angry feelings, we are not only in an uncomfortable mindset, but we also run the risk of making poor communication decisions that might sorely affect important future relationships.

And because of this poor mindset, the cravings for our substance will become loud in our minds in which relapse will be right around the corner. We need to quiet our minds so that the contention mind frame will quiet down as well. After all, our best mood comes forth when we are not tied to anything.

KILL THE RESENTMENTS

The resentments in our mind can be replaced by beautiful literature; they can be replaced by the poetry and wisdom that can only be found in the scriptures. Be one who studies the scriptures often, and you will find yourself forgiving often.

If our minds get twisted up in a resentment knot, then it's tough to hear the truth that comes from the Spirit. "Wherefore, it speaketh of things as they really are, and of things as they really will be" (Jacob 4:13).

So many of today's problems are communication problems. If someone snubbed us in public or took advantage of us in some way, we have to let it roll off our backs like water on a duck. We must give people the benefit of the doubt and realize that they are imperfect human beings just as we are.

Everyone seems to be comparing themselves to others nowadays, and it's especially bad with the emergence of Facebook and Instagram. We cannot let social media cause us to compare and grow prideful. We have to make the choice to not compare nor compete with everyone else's pride. "For jealousy is the rage of a man: therefore he will not spare in the day of vengeance" (Proverbs 6:34).

Remember, if we are getting mad and always feeling sorry for ourselves, then our mood will be one that is sorry and all over the place as well. We have to realize that no one owes us anything and that we aren't as special as we might think. The disease will scream that we are special and different and that our life is much harder than others'. In reality, everyone's life is hard—not just ours. Stop comparing and serve!

CONCLUSION

God is forgiving of our faults, and He expects us to be forgiving as well. If you think about it, we are all just a group of imperfect people living here upon this earth, trying to figure out how to make it in the School of Addiction. Once we capture this forgiveness mindset, then we can find our lives being filled with more joy, peace, sobriety, and lasting happiness.

CLASS 10
SEARCHER

"Wherefore, I beseech of you, brethren, that ye should search diligently in the light of Christ that ye may know good from evil; and if ye will lay hold upon every good thing, and condemn it not, ye certainly will be a child of Christ."
Moroni 7:19

The drug and alcohol scene of today is quite different from the scene of yesterday. In today's world, everybody supposedly has an injury which has caused pain clinics to sweep over the land. Doctors then write massive scripts to those unfortunate souls who have convinced themselves, and the doctor, that they are in pain when that couldn't be further from the truth. In my opinion, there are not many people on this earth who are candidates for maxed out scripts of time released OxyContin, Roxycontin, Xanax for anxiety, and Ambien to sleep. It seems reasonable to me that the only people who should be getting this amount of medication refilled each month should be the terminally ill cancer patient whose quality of life needs to be improved before they die, but what do I know—I'm not a doctor, but just a regular old recovering drug addict.

CHRONIC PAIN

A report released by the National Institute of Health stated, "It's time that treatment of chronic pain moves from a 1-pill-fits-all mindset to an evidence-based, individualized, multidisciplinary model that recognizes the value of non-pharmacological approaches, including physical therapy" (Blue Ridge Orthopaedic & Spine Center, "Physical Therapy offers a non-drug alternative to Pain Management," January 19, 2015).

Chronic pain affects an estimated 100 million Americans. Although numerous treatments are available for treatment of chronic pain, an estimated 5 to 8 million Americans use opioids for long-term management of chronic pain. There has been a dramatic increase in opioid prescriptions and use over the past 20 years. In 1991, the number of prescriptions written for opioids was 76 million, and in 2011 this number reached 219 million—wow! (National Institute of Health, "Pathways to Prevention Workshop: The Role of Opioids in the Treatment of Chronic Pain," September 2014).

It seems as if the only way to treat pain nowadays is through an opiate instead of some other holistic way through physical therapy, strength and conditioning, or even good nutrition practices. But let's be honest, we addicts don't care to be treated the holistic way anyway; because in all reality we take the opiates to alleviate stress and to break up the monotony of boring old life. It feels so good to have something in our pockets that can give way to a head change that numbs us out during those tasks that aren't so fun. Or, to know that we can just sit around and be lazy human beings without ever being challenged with the normal pressures and stresses that come when living in a competitive world.

PAINKILLERS AND INJURIES

Hospital admissions for prescription painkillers have increased more than fivefold in the last two decades. Yet evidence also indicates that 40–70% of people with chronic pain are not receiving proper medical treatment. The report found that the prevalence of chronic pain and the increasing use of opioids have created a "silent epidemic" of distress, disability, and danger to a large percentage of Americans (National Institute of Health, "Pathways to Prevention Workshop: The Role of Opioids in the Treatment of Chronic Pain," September 2014).

This large percentage of Americans are prescribed massive amounts of pills by a doctor; those pills are then spread out into the world and end up in junior highs, high schools, colleges, and the career world. Because, after all, with such big scripts, surely there are plenty left over to sell.

And then, when the pills become far too expensive, the consumer then makes their way to putting heroin into their system since it is far cheaper. Pretty sad.

THE WEIGHT ROOM AND GOALS

As kids, we jumped, ran, played, and even sweated each and every day. As adults, we stopped sweating, and we don't run and play anymore, which leaves us with a dark mind that seeks after the easy escape from reality. Now we bend over and our back goes out because we've gotten soft and out of shape, which then leads us into the doctor in search of today's only so-called treatment option—opiates.

I bet most people would be healed of their mind struggles and physical problems if they would just implement fitness and good nutrition practices into their lives. The weight room as a whole, with its accompanying barbell lifts and practices in mobility, can lead an individual to gain an improvement in their posterior chain strength (back, hamstrings, gluteus, quadriceps, abdominal). And when one improves their posterior chain strength, then their back health improves as well (see Mark Rippetoe, *Starting Strength: A Simple and Practical Guide for Coaching Beginners* [Wichita Falls: Aasgaard Company, 2005]).

I know this to be true because I have worked with hundreds of people who have come to me with so-called back problems and quickly found out that their back wasn't as bad as they or their doctor thought—and that they didn't need to be on pills.

I've had back surgery, and it was the weight room that brought my physical self back to life. There is no doubt that the lifts of the squat, deadlift, and pressing movements need to be performed properly, which is why it's important that you be taught how to do them by someone who has spent time on them—a qualified fitness professional.

The weight room can give us something to practice each day because it will be linked to our goals. We may set the goal of being able to squat four hundred pounds, and when we do finally achieve our goal, we can look back and be proud of ourselves for having the discipline to accomplish such a feat. We can look back and see the hours of time spent within the gym and how it helped us to stay clear, healthy, happy, and out of harm's way.

THE HOLISTIC APPROACH TO DEALING WITH PAIN

Let's be honest: everyone could lay the claim to having back pain, but some deal with it far better than others. Some wake up in the morning and choose not to jump to conclusions when they feel lower back tightness, while others dramatize their back pain and automatically seek after the pill instead of just relaxing and waiting for their body to get loose as the day moves on.

So many of our injuries (back and neck seem to be the most common excuse) could be healed if one would participate in good nutrition practices. The constant intake of high amounts of sugar leads the body to being chronically inflamed. And when the body is experiencing systemic inflammation or full-body inflammation, it has trouble repairing itself since the immune system will be spread entirely too thin. If you brought down your sugar intake and started exercising and getting stronger, your back and entire body inflammation would quiet down, leaving you with no excuse as to why you need to be on pills (Dallas and Melissa Hartwig, *It Starts With Food* [Las Vegas: Victory Belt Publishing, 2014]). And remember, we don't take pills for pain anyway, but only to escape from stress, so quit lying to yourself.

Therefore, make nutrition a part of your spiritual work by preparing healthy food within your home; and then sit down to enjoy it by eating slowly so that the digestion process can happen in the proper way. Don't be stimulated in any other direction except, of course, by your study of the scriptures that you are slowly reading as you are chewing and appreciating your food. A reverent and slow food practice promotes good food hygiene (Dallas and Melissa Hartwig, *It Starts With Food* [Las Vegas: Victory Belt Publishing, 2014]).

And then we will sleep better because of our healthy nutrition, which means waking up in the morning will become a brighter experience. We are now eating on a schedule and are organized not only with our food, but our overall life has become more organized ever since we placed the emphasis on organizing our food and health. Our cravings to escape are down as well because of our discipline with nutrition. Besides, there is no room for the escape anymore within our healthy routine of eating healthy, exercise, prayer, scripture study, listening to conference talks, attending church and addiction recovery meetings, and service to others, among much more.

GETTING OFF OPIATES

It's seems that the only way for people to get off opiates is to want it so badly that finding God becomes their only option. If a person won't find God, then they won't find the strength to get off opiates, period! Some may escape its grips for a time without finding God, but almost always these same people end up going back out for another round. After all, rock bottom can always get deeper until one is finally laid down in the casket.

That is why it's important to allow Jesus Christ to be your higher power instead of something that can't hold you accountable, like a rock, or even nature. These are all good things to have as a higher power, but they are not great higher powers. I had one young man tell me that his dead dog was his higher power, which was good for him, but not great for him. It seems to me that the only way a higher power works is if it's able to hold you accountable for the way that you acted. Again, Christ has a set of commandments that He has asked us to follow; and when we break those commandments, we feel saddened, contrite, and eventually a loss of His Spirit, which then motivates us to get His Spirit of charity back in our system so that we can feel safe again.

In the Book of Mormon, the prophet Alma taught the people of Zarahemla that the Lord "doth not dwell in unholy temples; neither can filthiness or anything which is unclean be received into the kingdom of God" (Alma 7:21).

So why stay on opiates when doing so will lead you nowhere in life other than the pawn shops, jail, or even death? Yes, you could look at it as being one more time, but one more time will lead to another year of use, which will be more wasted time in the tunnel of opiates.

Our thirties will become forties real fast; and our forties will become fifties even faster. And what a sad life it will become for the one who stays in hiding behind a substance for the majority of their life. By this time, family members will have written you off because you will have exhausted them of their resources and capacity to care anymore.

These are hard realities to accept. I know, because I have experienced them firsthand. However, there is always time to change no matter how long you've been out running.

Blood, sweat, and tears are what it takes to get off of opiates, but let's not pretend that it's impossible. Imagine yourself passing through the dope sickness and on to finding God; to then walking His 12 steps of repentance, jogging, reading, lifting weights, getting into prayer, and eating healthy. Envision yourself doing this for an entire year and imagine the type of person you would become. People would respect how far you've come. You would be getting comments from your peers on how well you looked and how proud they were of you. But such a vision only stays a vision if you have not the courage, nor the work ethic, to make it all happen. It's going to hurt to change, but why would you be given an opportunity to be inspiring in the lives of others if it were going to be easy? Nobody becomes inspired when they have witnessed someone do something that is easy. Be one who inspires!

SEARCH FOR SPIRITUAL EXPERIENCES

It should not be uncommon for us to spend part of our Saturday or Sunday at a track and field jogging and sprinting, followed by reading, prayer, and a nap in the shade of a tree. I always tell people that when I'm at peace with myself, you will find me taking naps under trees. When we are in the runaround for drugs and alcohol, there seems to be no time for track work, reading, or even naps; but while we are sober, the reverence of a track seems nice and relaxing. Make tracks a part of your life, and I promise you will find peace and sobriety.

Or we can get into road biking or mountain biking. How cool would it be to buy our first mountain bike—to be able to explore the mountains in a way that is fast paced, where we could stop often to look out over the valley and feel accomplished for making it to the top unbroken and without stopping. We might even say a prayer at the top that leads us to thoughts of sending out a thank-you text or making a call to that someone we have been meaning to call but haven't.

Such experiences will then lead us to learn about aerobic training and what it feels like physically and mentally to jog, bike, or hike for a long distance while changing up the intensity, terrain, and distance every so often. Sometimes we may find ourselves in a mind argument about whether we should quit because of the pain, or if we should press forward. When we do press forward, we will gain confidence and self-esteem, which is what's needed in order to switch from the path of self-pity and doubt to the rock-solid trail of faith and hope.

During these experiences, we can again search for God and thoughts of gratitude that will help us envision ourselves in a positive light. All of this will happen with the help of uplifting music, audiobooks, and conference talks.

We can search for uplifting music that can pull our mood out of the shadows. Put in your headphones and escape into a walk, jog, or drive, and watch what happens to your thinking. You just may find yourself calling that someone for whom you carried resentment, or sending out that thank-you text to someone who has helped you along the way. Be creative! Have the courage to go and explore places that will lead you to beautiful thinking, such as a river parkway, an old neighborhood, a mountain trail, or out in the country. Again, let music and walking help you to find a better vision of yourself.

Music can lead us to find nostalgia, and nostalgia feels good. So we should search for nostalgia through music and places of old so that our thinking can travel backward to the times when we were innocent and free, which was more than likely when we were children.

We can search for our childlike innocence by kicking a ball, shooting some hoops, playing catch; and if we have children, we should do it all with them so that we can help them build a set of healthy memories to lean on for when they are our age and may need them as we needed them.

SEARCH AFTER OUR TALENTS

Jesus told the story of a master who gave each of his three servants a sum of money. The amounts were set according to each servant's previously demonstrated capabilities. The man then left for a long time. When he returned, he asked each of these servants to report what he had done with the money.

The first two servants revealed they had doubled his investment. "Well done, thou good and faithful servant: thou hast been faithful over a few things, I will make thee ruler over many things: enter thou into the joy of thy lord," was the master's reply (Matthew 25:21; see also Matthew 25:23).

The third servant then came trembling before his master. He had already heard what the others had reported and knew that he could not give a similar report. "I was afraid," the servant said, "and went and hid thy talent in the earth" (Matthew 25:25). The master was upset. "Thou wicked and slothful servant," he said. Then he commanded, "Take therefore the talent from him, and give it unto him which hath ten talents." (Matthew 25:26, 28).

The Savior then gave the interpretation of the parable: Those who obtain other talents receive more talents in abundance. But those who do not obtain other talents shall lose even the talents they had initially (see Matthew 25:28–29; see also Ronald A. Rasband, "Parables of Jesus: The Parable of the Talents," *Liahona*, August 2003).

We get one shot at performing well in this life. And when we die and find out that we didn't do our best, then I imagine that to be Hell. There's no worse feeling than knowing that we didn't get the most out of our God-given talents. Imagine when God calls us out and tells us He's disappointed in us for how we performed in the game of life.

The parable of the ten virgins teaches that when the Lord comes, only half of all followers of Christ that are invited to the wedding feast will be given entrance. "For they that are wise and have received the truth, and have taken the Holy Spirit for their guide, and have not been deceived—verily I say unto you, they shall not be hewn down and cast into the fire, but shall abide the day" (D&C 45:57). The other half will be halted at the door due to them not being prepared. We can't just hear it, but we must act on what we've heard by walking the 12 steps of repentance.

This is not to scare you—it is to motivate you to use your talents wisely. You are wasting your time and talents if you stay on opiates.

CONCLUSION

We can search to eliminate stress in our lives by implementing better lifestyle practices. Is our life fulfilling? Do we feel like we have purpose? How often are we serving others? What are those things that are causing us to be unhappy? How are our family and friend relationships? Do we know God anymore?

These are all questions we should ask ourselves often, because if we wake up every day and are miserable with who we are, then we must replace the negative with a positive. If after work we find ourselves in the bottle, then what is the stress that's leading us to the bottle? Why can't we be led to the gym or out and about doing productive and healthy activities? If we are unhappy with the way we look and feel, obviously this is a huge stressor, so we must do something about it. If we hate our job, then we should do something about it by investing in ourselves so that we can eventually do what we love. The human species seems to be lazy and impatient. If we can find ourselves in the practice of putting a constant pressure toward our goals, then one day we will achieve those goals; and if we are working toward our goals, then our life has purpose and meaning anyway, and our stress will be down. Find out your priorities, create some goals, and then work hard to achieve those goals.

CLASS 11
ENDURANCE

"Behold, I am the law, and the light. Look unto me, and endure to the end, and ye shall live; for unto him that endureth to the end will I give eternal life."

3 Nephi 15:9

In the game of life, "the Lord seeth fit to chasten his people; yea, he trieth their patience and their faith" (Mosiah 23:21).

As enrollees in the School of Addiction, none of us can escape the adverse events that lay ahead. Things are going to happen throughout our recovery that will cause us to ask the question "Why me?" And if we do not carry the gospel of Jesus Christ's "perfect brightness of hope" (2 Nephi 31:20), then we will wallow in self-pity and feel victimized.

Everyone wants to hurry through the School of Addiction courses because of how uncomfortable they can become. You can't expect to be on top so quickly when you've been on the bottom for so long. Can you? Any school takes persistence and dedication in order to pass, and it is no different in the School of Addiction. In fact, this special school takes far more work than any other school because the development of Christ-like attributes is no easy feat.

Peter wrote, "Beloved, think it not strange concerning the fiery trial which is to try you, as though some strange thing happened unto you" (1 Peter 4:12).

The prophet Moroni confirmed our need to endure through adversity: "Dispute not because ye see not, for ye receive no witness until after the trial of your faith (Ether 12:6).

Therefore, we need to come to the realization that we might not always get what we were expecting and that the timetable might be longer than we had hoped for, which will be quite the challenge since instant gratification is what we are used to experiencing. There is no instant gratification in the School of Addiction, but only slow results that come "in process of time" (Moses 7:21) from putting a consistent pressure on a healthy way of life, even Christ's way of life.

Paul observed, "Now no chastening for the present seemeth to be joyous, but grievous: nevertheless afterward it yieldeth the peaceable fruit of righteousness" (Hebrews 12:11). After all, the best players in the game are those who remain meek and poised when adversity strikes since they see all tough experiences as being an opportunity to learn and grow. The Lord even said, "He that endureth to the end, the same shall be saved" (2 Nephi 31:15).

THE FATHER AND THE SON PATIENTLY ENDURED

Even from the beginning, Christ was the perfect example of how to endure. He was born in a manger since there was "no room . . . in the inn" (Luke 2:7). And for most of His mortal ministry "the Son of Man [had] not where to lay his head" (Matthew 8:20). Christ was therefore homeless.

Think about it! The humblest and meekest man to have ever walked the earth suffered the most. We can take comfort in knowing that our little mind struggles and addictions are nothing when compared to the vinegar and gall He was given to drink (Matthew 27:34).

The Lord is clear in the scriptures about how He works "in process of time" (Moses 5:19), "line upon line, precept upon precept" (D&C 98:12), and "here a little, and there a little" (Isaiah 28:10). Such concepts by the Lord tell us that we are to be patient chippers in this life and that when life becomes stale and monotonous, then we should be patient some more, and keep chipping away at living the Lord's lifestyle of health.

When we are patient, we allow the Lord to change us and do not get frustrated with Him. Such frustration by us more or less shows that we are still trying to be in control instead of allowing the Lord to control us. And though He will not rob us of our free agency, He will implant within us the great "Comforter, which shall teach him the truth and the way whither [we] shall go" (D&C 79:2), therefore increasing the peace in our souls and helping us to be meek and submissive, which are both cousins to patience.

The Lord has an incredible amount of patience for us in the School of Addiction, which is why we are to be patient as we live on His timetable. Our Heavenly Father holds faithfully to His commitment of allowing us to be free agents in this life, which is not only a great sign of love by Him, but is an act of service since He allows us to find our way through heartaches, failure, loss, and, of course, disappointments, all while working other angles on our behalf so that our prayers can be answered by Him. The Lord has counseled us in the Doctrine and Covenants that we should use our agency to do good, "For the power is in them, wherein they are agents unto themselves. And inasmuch as men do good they shall in nowise lose their reward" (D&C 58:28).

What patience and endurance it must've taken for our Heavenly Father to allow His Only Begotten Son to suffer the torments of an evil world and to take upon Him the sins of the world so that His cross could set the world free.

"And my Father sent me that I might be lifted up upon the cross; and after that I had been lifted up upon the cross, that I might draw all men unto me, that as I have been lifted up by men even so should men be lifted up by the Father, to stand before me, to be judged of their works" (3 Nephi 27:14).

"Then said Jesus unto his disciples, If any man will come after me, let him deny himself, and take up his cross, and follow me" (Matthew 16:24).

What beautiful examples of sharing, sacrifice, and patience in order to enact a plan of salvation that would take the sting out of death and allow for all people to experience a reuniting of body and spirit after they have given up the ghost in this life (Mark 15:37).

And if Christ had not risen from the dead, or have broken the bands of death that the grave should have no victory, and that death should have no sting, there could have been no resurrection.

But there is a resurrection, therefore the grave hath no victory, and the sting of death is swallowed up in Christ (Mosiah 16:7–8).

Neal A. Maxwell explained, "Christ's victory over death ended the human predicament. Now there are only personal predicaments, and from these too we may be rescued by following the teachings of him who rescued us from general extinction" (*The Neal A. Maxwell Quote Book*, [West Valley City: Bookcraft, 1997], 287).

PATIENCE AND DILIGENCE

We must, then, be patient with the healing process of the Atonement. "Therefore God himself atoneth for the sins of the world, to bring about the plan of mercy, to appease the demands of justice, that God might be a perfect, just God, and a merciful God also" (Alma 42:15). It is not a process that is loud and noticeable in the everyday moments, but is one that lays in our reflection from having patiently endured through our mind struggles by feasting on the Lord's word and lifestyle with an unwavering diligence. "But they that wait upon the Lord shall renew their strength; they shall mount up with wings as eagles; they shall run, and not be weary; and they shall walk, and not faint" (Isaiah 40:31).

I remember when I was first trying to change my life. I had gotten into a good habit of praying, reading, eating healthy, going to church, and training in the gym; and I remember asking God, in what was a beautiful prayer experience, to help me keep being diligent and consistent in my efforts in trying to change because I was somewhat on the fence of keeping it all up. "Seek me diligently and ye shall find me; ask, and ye shall receive; knock, and it shall be opened unto you" (D&C 88:63).

I remember getting off my knees and feeling like there was no doubt at all that I was going to be able to keep it up. And I have ever since, even though I have stumbled many times through relapse. Doesn't keeping it up mean fighting through relapse as well?

Some years back, I had a major relapse and was quite low on myself because I had been doing so well. However, I fought back and was led to a deeper study in the School of Addiction. Because of that relapse, I found myself being recommitted to the Church's addiction recovery meetings (ARP meetings), which before that relapse I had been going through the motions and hardly ever attending. Since I had been humbled once again, a great learning experience then came my way in the School of Addiction. What a blessing!

Think about it! If God was going to have me be a coach in the School of Addiction, I needed to learn about those circle meetings. Therefore, that relapse may have been just what I needed. Without it, I wouldn't have been humble enough to begin a serious study of the course. That is why in this book I've been asking for you to be open so that you don't have to make the same mistakes that I did of not being open to something that is good and beautiful. Many people say that those meetings cause them to crave, but anything can make us crave, so that isn't a good excuse. If you're saying stuff like this, then all you are really saying is that you want to do it your way, and not the head coach's way. Remember, all students will get lost in a course without some guidance. We cannot do it our way, nor can we do it alone.

ENDURE THROUGH MONEY STRUGGLES

Most of us are in a bad position financially because of our addictions. What I've learned is that if we continue to do poorly in the School of Addiction, then we will continue to do poorly with our money. We can't expect to hop into a high-paying job when we haven't invested in our ourselves properly, can we? What I mean by this is that if we had been high and clouded for some time, then we were obviously on pause with our character. Therefore, we are not that competent to be making money. Why is our Head Coach going to provide us with an easy way to make money when for so long we showed him that we couldn't do the right thing with it?

I believe that wealth and stability can come to all of us at some point, though we must be willing to start at the bottom and make our way slowly to the top. When I say slowly, I mean just that—SLOWLY! Generally, we all want "things" now. However, we may have to endure for five-plus years of making correct choices and working hard on our character before we can start creating some wealth and stability for ourselves. It's immature to think that we are to be owed anything or that it will be easy, because it isn't. It can't be, or else we wouldn't learn how to appreciate money and stability, nor would we learn anything about endurance in the School of Addiction.

In the School of Addiction, we are asked to patch up the holes of our character so that we cannot only stay sober but so that we can be an asset to somebody or something. Going into the job interview with little character is like the bucket that looks okay on the outside but leaks water on the inside. It's only a matter of time before the holes in our character will become exposed, which is why we must go to work at improving our character so that we can improve our self-worth and value. And we will improve our character the most if we will study, with a passion, the doctrines of the gospel of Jesus Christ.

Consider again what President Boyd K. Packer of the Quorum of the Twelve Apostles said about the power that true doctrine has in helping individuals improve their character:

> True doctrine, understood, changes attitudes and behavior. The study of the doctrines of the gospel will improve behavior quicker than a study of behavior will improve behavior. Preoccupation with unworthy behavior can lead to unworthy behavior. That is why we stress so forcefully the study of the doctrines of the gospel. ("Little Children," *Ensign*, November 1986)

QUITTING FRIENDS AND INVESTING IN YOURSELF

Quitting drugs and alcohol often means quitting friends, which can be a hard thing to do. It makes sense, however, that you must quit hanging out with those friends who have the same poor habits as you, or your habits will never go away. Again, it all depends on who you want to be in this life. And if you want to hang out with the crew in the parking lot instead of going to class, then be my guest—but don't come back complaining five years from now when you haven't made any progress. Get out of the parking lot and go to class!

Why not go back to a university setting and endure through school so you can obtain a degree that will look good on a resume? Find out what you want to study and then stick with it until you are done with school. How cool it is to be walking on a university campus wearing a backpack and working toward something that could possibly bring you long-term stability. You might find a passion for your university studies, which will be a new focus for you, and one that is now far away from your old poor focus of using.

OUR POOR ATTENTION SPAN

Many people in the School of Addiction struggle with their attention spans, which is a flaw they lean on as an excuse. Yes, attention deficit disorder is real, but that doesn't mean you can't do anything without taking a drug to enhance your performance.

Adderall has become the drug of our day that supposedly leads people who have ADD to being more productive and smarter. This drug, when ingested, tells the mind that we are capable of anything. Tasks that we couldn't stay on task for are now interesting and enjoyable. However, what goes up must surely come down, leaving us with a mindset that is far from positive.

A study performed by Johns Hopkins Bloomberg School of Public Health showed that while the number of prescriptions for the stimulant Adderall has remained unchanged among young adults, misuse and emergency room visits have risen dramatically. The study examined trends from 2006 through 2011 and found that it is mainly 18- to 25-year-olds who are inappropriately taking Adderall without a prescription, primarily getting the medication from family and friends.

"The growing problem is among young adults," says study coauthor Ramin Mojtabai, MD, MPH, PhD, a professor of mental health at the Bloomberg School.

> In college, especially, these drugs are used as study-aid medication to help students stay up all night and cram. Our sense is that a sizeable proportion of those who use them believe these medications make them smarter and more capable of studying. We need to educate this group that there could be serious adverse effects from taking these drugs and we don't know much at all about their longterm health effects. (Benham, Barbara, and JH Bloomberg School of Public Health. "Adderall Misuse Rising Among Young Adults," Johns Hopkins Bloomberg School of Public Health. N.p., 17 Feb. 2016).

I have ADD, and for me, I have learned that it is a gift and a curse. Oftentimes, the disorder presses on me to the point where I'm uncomfortable because I feel like I can't get anything done. Then the thought to take something to help me get something done pops into my head, which seems to feed the addiction cycle. However, if we will just lean on God for inspiration, then "[He] will send [us] the Comforter, which shall teach [us] the truth and the way whither [we] shall go" (D&C 79:2).

Everyone can lean on the idea that they have a hard time concentrating and focusing. No one likes to write papers or do busy work regardless of whether they have ADD or not. Yes, some people can stay on task longer than others, but these others must find a way to be productive without putting amphetamines, opiates, or whatever into their system in an effort to enhance their performance. If you struggle with sitting in an office—well then, don't take the career path that leads you to sitting in an office. Go the route of becoming a firefighter, teacher, construction worker, or a coach of some sort. Many of us will need to be in the service of others in order to stay sober, so take the career path that allows you to work with people.

Of course, we all have to do things that we don't like to do early on, but those things don't have to be our end-state goals. Chip away at those little stepping stone tasks so that later on down the road you can do what you love. But remember, if you remain on high amounts of amphetamines to try and get ahead, then your life will go in a big circle instead of heading upwards on the "strait and narrow path" (Helaman 3:29).

HOLD TO THE IRON ROD

In the Book of Mormon, the word of God is referred to as an iron rod. In interpreting his father's dream for his brothers, Nephi wrote,

> And they said unto me: What meaneth the rod of iron which our father saw, that led to the tree?
> And I said unto them that it was the word of God; and whoso would hearken unto the word of God, and would hold fast unto it, they would never perish; neither could the temptations and the fiery darts of the adversary overpower them unto blindness, to lead them away to destruction. (1 Nephi 15:23–24)

I have found that if I hold tight to Christ's gospel (the iron rod), I will become who and what God wants me to become in this life. But if I lose hold of the iron rod, then I will remain a drug addict who relies only on amphetamines and opiates for support instead of God. The choice is mine. This choice is also yours.

Remember, we only grow when we are involved in those tasks that cause us to feel discomfort. If we are always escaping the discomfort, then the learning experience will escape us as well. We've got to be able to sit down and endure through the monotony of life's boring paperwork so that we can appreciate the breaks in the sun. The long hard work week that is full of stress, but also sobriety, will lead us to feel a great joy and appreciation for the upcoming weekend. But if we escaped the entire work week by way of amphetamines, then what's the difference between the work week and the weekend?

ENDURE THROUGH CRAVINGS

When cravings come into the mind, endure through them. Do not let the thought travel too far on down the road, but stop it right away. Yes, your peace will be tainted, but not for long if you will get moving. You won't feel like moving or doing anything, but if you have the courage, then you will "come off conqueror" (D&C 10:5). Go run sprints, run a mile for time, go hard in a conditioning workout within the gym, pray, read, listen to conference talks, and do everything possible to feed the Light of Christ into your mind. Every time I have had the courage to go and make something physical and spiritual happen during a craving, I have found success one hundred percent of the time. When I haven't had the courage, then I haven't found success, in which I found myself being caught back up in the runaround. Learn to endure through cravings, and don't jump to conclusions. Slow down, take a few deep breaths, and go right into talking with God. Think about it! You don't want to screw up the peace you've been feeling, so stay on the path you are on so that you don't have to feel scared tomorrow.

THE LONG HAUL

We have to be in it for the long haul. We cannot be in it for the short game and expect long-term results. Each day, we must strive to capture balance. We must eat healthily, read some powerful literature, exercise, attend our meetings, and make it all happen in our professional and family lives. This seems to be a daunting and busy day for many, but it's actually the day of a progressive and happy individual. There is so much beauty in the recovery process. In this process, you have the opportunity to capture spiritual experiences daily; to read, study, and pray to God; and to share in beautiful conversations with others. In this process, we get the opportunity to participate in truly honest conversations with others. We get to talk about the deep things of God. We get to talk about our relationships. We get to talk about our fears, weaknesses, and insecurities. We get to hug it out. We get to make brand new friends with people who truly understand what we are going through. We get to become inspiring in the lives of others. And finally, we get the opportunity to become coaches in the School of Addiction.

We can get addicted to this beautiful recovery process. Eventually, we can be thankful that we had our eyes opened to such a beautiful way of life. If we wouldn't have gotten wrapped up in a substance, then we wouldn't have had to fight so hard to capture spiritual experiences. We wouldn't have had to go on long walks in an effort to capture scenic views that could cause us to feel gratitude for our Savior; we wouldn't have had to fight for a brand-new perspective on life; we wouldn't have had to build our character in such a way as to have the new ability to abstain from those substances that bring the fast pleasure.

CONCLUSION

I just recently went through the Mormon temple with my family and had a wonderful spiritual experience that has since led me to slow down even more in my mind. I'm learning that with me going to the temple each week to perform in a sacred work, and by studying often, that I am able to experience joy in living the simple way of life. I'm realizing that if I choose to go back out and pick up those pills, then my life will become chaotic once again, causing me to feel as if the entire world is caving in on me. However, if I keep my spiritual condition high by living the commandments and staying lowly, reverent, and meek, then I will stay feeling safe and won't feel the need to invite the chaos back into my life. I have found that I like how I am around my wife and kids when I have the Holy Ghost dwelling within my system. I pray that I can keep this Spirit with me always. I want to teach my kids how to use the Spirit in their own lives so that they can make their way safely past the shiny objects that lay on the world's roadside. I also want this for you.

Spending eternity with my family is my motivation nowadays. I don't want to be running around and looking for the easy way out of the game anymore. I want to stay competing with myself so that at the end of my life I am ready to "be judged [for my] works" (3 Nephi 27:14).

So enjoy the ride, even though the ride is long and oftentimes hurts. And at the end of each day, we should be talking to God on how we did, and what we need to fix. And if we do this each day, we will be able to endure a little longer since we will be carrying "the mind of Christ" (1 Corinthians 2:16).

CLASS 12

CRAVINGS

"For the natural man is an enemy to God, and . . . will be, forever and ever, unless he . . . and putteth off the natural man and becometh a saint through the atonement of Christ the Lord."

Mosiah 3:19

Why is it that we can be doing so well but then quickly be doing so bad? Why do we choose to not stay in the peace of sobriety but instead choose to go back out into the chaos of our addiction?

It's always hard to talk about relapse because no one wants relapse to happen, nor do we want anyone to think that it's okay to relapse just because we are talking about it. But to be truthful, relapse happens more often than not.

It's our reservations that seem to keep us in it. The one who is in jail and is forced to stay sober has the reservation of coming out of jail to get high because he thinks he can handle it just "one more time." It's almost like these individuals have to get sober twice: once when they were forced in jail, but another when they are free to choose again on the outside.

ESCAPE PLAN

When we have allowed the wrong thought to travel too far and are in the middle of a craving, we must then search for something else to look forward to that can get us high naturally. The reason for the craving in the first place was probably due to us being bored, stressed, and depressed with nothing to look forward to. The spiritual high that comes from living on Christ's foundation can give us a charitable, peaceful character that everyone likes, including ourselves. And "when the devil shall send forth his mighty winds . . . it shall have no power over you to drag you down to the gulf of misery . . . because of the rock upon which ye are built (Helaman 5:12).

Dallin H. Oaks gives this inspired counsel on how to beat a craving:

Humble disciples of Jesus Christ will gain the sensitivity to recognize the deep feelings, social situations, and physical surroundings that trigger the temptation to use pornography. Having analyzed those triggers, they will develop a personal escape plan to help them:
- Recognize triggers and cravings as they occur.
- Establish specific actions to help them withdraw from the temptation.
- Redirect thoughts and energy toward the Lord.
- Outline daily specific actions to fortify their personal commitment to live righteously.

(Dallin H. Oaks, "Recovering from the Trap of Pornography," *Liahona*, November 2015)

LOOK FORWARD TO HEALTH

By connecting our gospel spiritual work with exercise and nature, we will create new memories that can help us have something to look forward to. So now when our addiction tries to lead our thinking toward what it can offer, we can now offset the craving with the feelings of hope that the health of the gospel of Jesus Christ promises us, which are a peaceful, charitable character; exercising in nature while getting lost in inspirational music and prayer; reading and studying the scriptures in beautiful locations; and exercising at a high intensity while allowing our endorphins to lift our mind frame up and over the craving to be "cast out" (Revelation 12:9).

Therefore, we have to be able to look forward to something that is just as powerful as our addiction thoughts. We have always relied on the temporary pleasures that our addiction offered us. Now, we can look forward to a progression in our character taking place as we allow the Holy Spirit to help us find success in choosing the right over wrong and realizing that we will be blessed with further strength and abundance the better we get at putting "off the natural man" (Mosiah 3:19).

What about looking forward to doing something with your life? What about trying to point your addiction in the way of finding success, stability, and even wealth, where we "seek [riches] for the intent to do good" (Jacob 2:19)? Those of us who struggle with addiction can be great in this life if we would just point our addictive mind in the right direction. We need to have a vision of who we want to become, and then we need to chip away at becoming that person. Now when we are in the midst of a craving, we can look forward to working on ourselves by living the lifestyle of Christ so that we can become that person we have always wanted to be. With this new angle of perspective, we will find our way around the craving because we will have something to look forward to, which will be the investment in our character so as to become like Jesus Christ. "For the Lord God hath said that: Inasmuch as ye shall keep my commandments ye shall prosper in the land" (2 Nephi 4:4).

LOOK FORWARD TO FEELING THE SPIRIT

When the fear of making a poor decision pops into our minds, it can be outshined by our effort to work on our charitable self, "for charity shall cover the multitude of sins" (1 Peter 4:8). With the help of the Holy Ghost, our addictive mind can be given inspired ideas of ways that we can be passionate about something—ideas of how we can create something out of nothing, thus pointing all of our addiction energy into a positive direction with hopes of it working for us instead of against us. If we do find something healthy to be passionate about, then we will likewise be passionate about making our way past the addict lifestyle for the duration—since we will have found something that is more powerful than our addiction. Therefore, it will be replaced with the health and happiness of the gospel of Jesus Christ.

Now, instead of always being in the battle between choosing right and wrong, we are now addicted to reading books written by modern-day prophets and apostles, studying the scriptures, exercising and eating healthily, and trying to live the commandments of the gospel. These truths found in our reading and in our practicing at living the health of the gospel keeps us further motivated to live in harmony with God's teachings. We now realize that all we have to do to find success and true happiness in this life is to develop an honest, God-fearing character that works harder than most. After all, being a hard worker is one of the gifts that came to us when we finally learned how to point our addiction in the right direction. "And if a person gains more knowledge and intelligence in this life through his diligence and obedience than another, he will have so much the advantage in the world to come" (D&C 130:19).

The thought to escape still travels into our mind, but we keep such thoughts on the surface of our thinking, never allowing them to burrow too deeply. Our physical self is in tune with our exercise, as is our nutritional and spiritual. The cravings for the world are no match for such a powerful harmonization because through this harmonization we can see our best self quickly developing. The glow of our soul is greater than it has ever been, and all who come in contact with us recognize this unique light. It motivates us to put off the loud yell of the world and to listen for the "still small voice" (1 Kings 19:12) of the Spirit. Clearer and clearer the spiritual whisper will develop, and softer and softer the world's whisper becomes until we have been "healed by him of [our] infirmities" (Luke 5:15) and are now innocent as we were when we were children.

LOOK FORWARD TO THE SIMPLE LIFE

Remember, it is inside the simple life where the greatest highs can be captured. The hugs from your children; the good conversation with your wife; the day of fishing with your father; the service project in your neighborhood; the good book; the good-sounding song that created happy emotions; the scenery while up on a mountain peak; the family vacation. These are all spiritual highs that are given to us by God but often aren't recognized as being spiritual highs since they aren't always linked to blissful experiences. In order to capture that scenery on the peak, you had to suffer on the hike. In order to get that hug from your children, you had to be patient when they were throwing temper tantrums. In order to finish that good book, you had to turn off the TV and make time for reading. In order to have that good conversation with your wife, you had to get rid of your selfishness. And in order to have that good experience with your dad on the river, you had to be living right so that you were in tune enough to appreciate such father-and-son moments.

The spiritual highs are linked to challenge, while the world's highs are not. The roller coaster type fun is impressive and great for the moment, but it doesn't last like the memory of hiking fifteen miles into the backcountry with a loaded pack. The 15-mile hike was a grind, but the campfire experience with your father, son, nephew, and brothers-in-law made it all worth it. That type of memory will never leave us, while the roller coaster type memories of us using and partying are fleeting at best, and won't matter one bit in the eternal scheme of things.

FIGHT THROUGH THE STORMY MIND

I have had so many times where the storm inside my head has felt nearly unbearable. Times when my stress levels and insecurities have gotten so bad that I felt like I might lose it. During these times of when I wanted to escape these tough feelings with the help of opiate, I just told myself that God would help me to roll with the punches, and He did. I felt Him encouraging me to go for a jog-walk to work on prayer while listening to my self-help audiobooks and inspirational music. Afterward, I felt empowered and free from the chains that were holding me down inside my mind. Hope came back, and before long I was calling my wife and letting her know that I loved her and that I was sorry for being emotionally vacant.

You have to be courageous and willing to feel some discomfort through burning legs and lungs if you want to escape the discomfort in your mind. The discomfort in your mind is the far worse experience, and I'm here to tell you that exercising in scenery while working on prayer and gratitude can free up your mind and will help you to start seeing things clearly. Now, you can go home and be you. Of course, your problems will still be there, but at least you can now see them clearly, without over-dramatizing them.

Go to a long hill and run up it as fast as you can; go on a hike up in the mountains while listening to a self-help audiobook; go for a jogging experience in an area that will help you to capture nostalgia; go run sprints at a track or on some grass. Do these things, and I promise, you will find a way to compete with your stresses and addictions. Be a competitor and quit leaning on the excuse of not having what it takes to change. The human spirit craves to experience excellence. And when we escape our feelings and stresses, then our spirit becomes saddened and less active. Let your addictive personality ignite your spirit by being a hard worker on finding health. Make it all happen!

WIN THE BATTLE AGAINST THE CRAVING

1. When the thought pops into your head, don't let it travel too far. Don't let the thought snowball out of control. Don't let yourself be unrealistic.

2. Ask for help through fervent prayer. Prayer should continue in your head constantly, believing that you will receive help through this challenging time. You have to believe that God has your best interest in mind, loves you, and wants you to succeed.

3. Search for gratitude and look to be thankful for all you have. When you are thankful for even the littlest of things, you become a better decision-maker. Being thankful will help you realize that happiness can be found in the simplest of things and that through these simple things you can overcome the craving. You realize that everything doesn't have to be fun in the way that Satan would have you believe, for it's through the simple things in life that the most joy can be obtained.

4. Think about all the progress you've made and the negative effects that the substance will give way to. Think about how temporary it will be and the depression associated with the choice to partake. Think about how deceitful Satan really is—and how he will take you to the top falsely and then drop you into a dark hole.

5. Get moving! Go experience a workout. Get your endorphins going naturally. You'd be surprised how physical fitness can get your mind back on track. The brain works best after an intense workout.

6. Call someone and let him or her know you are struggling. This helps take the pressure off you. If someone else knows, then you are less likely to go through with it. Chances are this person will be able to talk you out of it.

7. Work hard on your spirituality; look to find comfort and confidence through it. This can be accomplished through reading, prayer, and going to a spiritual place, such as church, the mountains, or any place that promotes peace and calmness. Nature can bring your soul closer to God.

8. Search for a calming sound through music. Search for music that uplifts the soul and heightens the mood. Search for music that will lead your thoughts back to your loving family. Search for music that will remind you of positive memories—memories of your innocence and even childhood. Search for music that invites the Spirit into your presence and then look to feel His love.

9. Endure. Wait it out, for it will end, and you will feel better soon. Don't get down on yourself by talking to yourself in a negative way. Envision yourself as a confident person who can overcome anything. Reassure yourself of how good you've been doing. You're not going to let Satan get you.

10. Win the WAR, for this is what the gospel of Jesus Christ has been preparing you for all along. Beat and overcome Satan. You are prepared. Now find the courage to put the gospel of Jesus Christ to use. You're in control—make it happen.

Let the gospel of Jesus Christ change you like it changed me. "Yea, blessed are the poor in spirit who come unto me, for theirs is the kingdom of heaven" (3 Nephi 12:3).

THE SCHOOL OF ADDICTION PRINCIPLES

1. We compete with ourselves every day by staying clear of drugs and alcohol. We are always striving to do the right thing and are okay with feeling contrite when we fall short.

2. We are hard workers in our homes, professional lives, and the gospel of Jesus Christ.

3. We listen to good audiobooks, conference talks, and healthy music, and watch a little healthy TV.

4. We hike and walk often while listening to music and audiobooks. We jog, sprint, and run hills often.

5. We lift weights and condition in both the aerobic and anaerobic energy systems.

6. We understand nutrition and do our best to eat as healthy as we can.

7. We pray often.

8.   We don't get offended and are not hardened against principles of truth.

9.   We help those who are in need and are not afraid to serve others.

10.   We are family oriented.

11.   We seek to obtain a meek, humble, and patient character. We carry quiet strength.

12.   We smile often and always seek to not let our moods get the best of us.

13.   We refrain from pornography because it will lead us to feeling hopeless and lowers our spiritual condition.

14.   We seek to have beautiful conversations with people, are good listeners, and are commendable.

15.   We send out healthy text messages and call to check on people often.

16.   We focus on staying present so we can eliminate resentments and contention; and we are forgiving of others and ourselves.

17.   We attend our church and addiction recovery meetings. We aren't afraid to tell our story.

18.   We stay active in the gospel of Jesus Christ of Latter-day Saints so that we can stay being good coaches in the School of Addiction.

19.   We realize that if we stop living the Gospel of Jesus Christ, we won't be any good at coaching.